Uncoverings
1989

Volume 10 of the Research Papers of the
American Quilt Study Group

edited by Laurel Horton

Copyright © 1990 by the
American Quilt Study Group.
All rights reserved.

Copyright note: This is a collective work. AQSG holds the copyright to this volume and any reproduction of it in whole. Rights to individual articles are held by the authors. Requests for permission to quote or reproduce material from any article should be addressed to the author.

Published by the American Quilt Study Group
660 Mission Street, Suite 400
San Francisco CA 94105
Manufactured in the United States

Uncoverings is indexed by the
Clothing and Textile Arts Index.

ISBN 1-877859-00-1
ISSN 0227-0628

Library of Congress catalog card number:
81-649486

Cover photo: Baltimore album quilt, inscribed "The Album presented to Mary Updegraf by H. H., 1850." Photograph courtesy of Christie's.

Contents

Preface   5

RESEARCH PAPERS

Eleanor Hamilton Sienkiewicz:
The Marketing of Mary Evans   7

Barbara Brackman: *Signature Quilts:
Nineteenth-Century Trends*   25

Suellen Meyer: *Early Influences of the Sewing Machine
and Visible Machine Stitching on Nineteenth-Century Quilts*   38

Elizabeth Weyrauch Shea and Patricia Cox Crews:
Nebraska Quiltmakers: 1870–1940   54

Debra Ballard: *The Ladies Aid of
Hope Lutheran Church*   69

Virginia Gunn: *Quilts for Milady's Boudoir*   81

Jane Przybysz: *The Body En(w)raptured:
Contemporary Quilted Garments*   102

Nancilu Burdick:
The Julia Boyer Reinstein Collection   123

Gail Andrews Trechsel: *Mourning Quilts in America*   139

SPECIAL PRESENTATION

Bets Ramsey: *A Tribute to Mariska Karasz*   159

Index   161

Preface

With this volume the American Quilt Study Group marks ten years of sponsorship of the presentation and publication of research on American quilts and quiltmakers. Someone unfamiliar with quilt research might think that all interesting aspects of the subject should be adequately covered by now, yet active researchers and their audiences become increasingly aware of additional topics which need to be investigated and reported.

As in previous years this volume encompasses a variety of subjects, perspectives, and methodologies. One theme that emerges from the essays as a group is the relationship between private and public aspects of quiltmaking. Although quilts are generally made privately by individuals or in small groups, the creation of those quilts is profoundly influenced by the changing world of fashion, international events, and industrial and corporate developments.

The essays span the time period from the early nineteenth century through the present, and they cover a geographic scope from the urban centers of the east coast to the rural Great Plains. Some authors address their research from an academic perspective, while others speak from the role of participant/observer.

Research—the systematic inquiry or investigation of a subject in order to discover or revise facts, theories, or applications—is most often associated with past events. Indeed, the passage of time usually allows us to review the past with detachment. However, some scholars focus on an examination of contemporary events, and their findings may seem controversial to today's audiences.

The American Quilt Study Group is proud to present the tenth volume of *Uncoverings*. We look forward to continued and expanded sponsorship of research into any and all aspects of quilts and quiltmaking in the future. AQSG gratefully acknowledges the generous contribution from the East Bay Heritage Quilters, of Albany, California, which helped fund the publication of *Uncoverings 1989*.

RESEARCH PAPERS

The Marketing of Mary Evans

Eleanor Hamilton Sienkiewicz

"I have a theory which cannot be proved," wrote the psychiatrist *cum* quilt expert, Dr. William Rush Dunton, Jr., (1868–1966) in his book *Old Quilts*. "An artist . . . made her living by making [Baltimore Album] quilts . . . [and she] acquired considerable local fame." This modest statement doesn't sound like the stuff of which myths are made, but in today's mercurial art world, watch—it may be happening. Mary who? Fewer people will ask that question this year than last, for the answer has been streamlined and packaged for popular consumption. Two books published in 1974 first tentatively suggested that Mary Evans might be just that needle artist whom Dr. Dunton sought. Today, fifteen years later, cautious speculation has given way to confident assertion. The word is out. Mary Evans was a "master quiltmaker," the "first professional quiltmaker."[1] Mary Evans supplied "prefabricated blocks for which she received payment" and signed "those blocks in standardized script with their donors' names."[2] Mary Evans seems to be the hottest selling quiltmaker of the mid-nineteenth century. Is it true? Did she really make the well more than a dozen quilts now popularly attributed to her in just half a dozen years? Here's the story—you be the judge.

Record quilt prices of five years ago look like bargains today as Americana prices escalate. On January 21, 1989, a Baltimore Album Quilt dated 1850 and described as "the work of Mary Evans . . . commissioned as a gift for Mary Updegraf by her wealthy family"[3] sold at Christie's auction in New York for $132,000. The same quilt appeared on the cover of E. P. Dutton's *Quilt Engagement Calendar 1984*. Thomas K. Woodard (of Thomas K. Woodard: American Antiques

---

Eleanor Hamilton Sienkiewicz, 5540 30th Street, N.W., Washington DC 20015.

and Quilts) told me that it had sold at the time of that publication for $26,000, so the 1989 sale shows more than a five-fold increase in roughly five years. At Sotheby's January 1987 Americana auction, another classic Baltimore Album Quilt sold for $176,000, and, according to its buyer, Frank J. Miele of Hirschl & Adler Folk, resold the same evening for "at least $200,000." In 1988, a classic Balitmore Album Quilt dated 1848, and inscribed "To John and Rebecca Chamberlain," with the maker listed as "probably Mary Evans"[4] sold for $110,000. In 1972, the *National Antiques Review* had pictured that same quilt and reported that at the Pennypacker Auction House in Kenhorst, Pennsylvania, "it surpassed everything else in beauty, interest, and price — $3,800."[5] In sixteen years, then, this classic Baltimore Album Quilt had increased in price roughly 3,000%.

Often presented as gifts, many Album Quilts have survived in remarkable condition, no doubt treated as art rather then as bedding. Album Quilts, which became popular in the 1840s and remained popular for several decades, seem to reflect the general Victorian mania for collecting things. Like albums of all sorts, these quilts house collections on a theme and were made along the Eastern seabord and, later, further west. In the Baltimore County area these Album Quilts emerged as a unique quilt genre because of their distinct artistic characteristics and their great numbers. As a writer and quiltmaker with a consummate interest in how, why, and by whom mid-ninteenth century Baltimore quilts were made, I frequently go to New York auctions and galleries to study these quilts on display.

January 21, 1989, was a Saturday quilt shoppers will remember. It was fur weather and antiques were in the air. Those who made the Christie's, Sotheby's, Winter Antiques Show[6] circuit quickly caught a theme: all three were offering Baltimore Album Quilts attributed to Mary Evans. "It's her! It's another quilt by Mary Evans!" I heard exclaimed for the third time. I had been standing awhile at the top of Sotheby's main staircase, making notes on the quilt "attributed to Mary Evans, Baltimore, Maryland, mid-19th Century."[7] When the young man added, "It's not as nice as the one that sold at Christie's this morning," I couldn't refrain from asking what the quilt at Christie's was like. He and his friend shared their catalog. The quilt in question was the Baltimore Album Quilt shown on the cover of the *Quilt Engagement Calendar 1984*. "And the one at the Winter Antiques Show," I asked. "Oh, it was much fancier than this one, but here, take this extra ticket if you like, we have to catch our plane back to Dallas." I had a train to catch, too, but there would be other trains.

My stopover at the Winter Antiques show was worth it. I recognized the quilt in America Hurrah's booth, this time from E. P. Dutton's *Quilt Engagement Calendar 1989* where its caption reads: "inscribed Ellenor [sic] and Elizabeth A. Gorsuch, ca. 1840, . . . many blocks . . . may confidently be attributed to the hand of Mary Evans." (Birth dates for Mary Evans are given variously as 1829 or 1830, making her ten or eleven years old in 1840. It is hard to imagine so young a child having made a piece of needle art of this magnitude, 108 inches x 108 inches in size, or in terms of time and materials.) The Gorsuch quilt was of Baltimore Album Quilt style and was labeled at the show as having descended in a Baltimore County family, with the date changed to "circa 1845." Such provenance alone makes it very valuable even without further specific attribution. "Sold," proprietor Joel Kopp replied to my fellow customer's query, "for a high five figure price. Over fifty and under one hundred."

The three Baltimore Album Quilts I saw offered that Saturday had all been advertised in print as "attributed to Mary Evans" or "made by Mary Evans—yet her name appeared on none of them. What is the origin of this attribution? The name "Mary Evans" was connected to the Baltimore Album Quilts in the mid-twentieth century by the quilt expert, Dr. William Rush Dunton, Jr., who had written "I have a theory which cannot be proved," and despite subsequent skillful research it remains unproven today. Her name doesn't appear on any Baltimore Album Quilts at all that we know of, yet it is this unproven attribution to Mary Evans which, unproven, is increasingly confidently asserted in the marketing of these quilts at the prices of upscale real estate. Thus, while the popularity of quilts as collectors' items is now well established, quilt authentication standards in the marketplace need to catch up.

Attribution to Mary Evans (for one unfinished appliqué block only) seems to have begun with a manuscript dated 1938 in "The Dunton Notebooks."[8] In 1974, Patsy and Myron Orlofsky[9] and Marilyn Bordes[10] published the first tentative references to Mary

Figure 1. The basted-only "City Springs block" photograph from the Dunton Notebooks, attributed to Mary Evans by her descendants. The block resurfaced in 1990 and is now in the collection of the Maryland Historical Society. Photo courtesy of The Baltimore Museum of Art.

Evans by name. They cite "The Dunton Notebooks" as their source. I went to the Baltimore Museum of Art to read for myself the reference to Mary Evans in these fragile old documents. The Notebooks—albums of notes, photos, clippings, and drawings—convey, in Volume VIII, that Evans Bramble (identified by Dena Katzenberg in *Baltimore Album Quilts* as Arthur Evans Bramble, Mary Evans's great-nephew) brought Dr. Dunton a set of seven quilt blocks.[11] One, a central medallion block depicting the City Springs, Dunton records through a photograph and a notation as "made by Miss Ford" (Mary Evans's married name). That attribution to her is contained in a seven-page written description of this set of blocks. The sophisticated City Springs block, which is only basted, is in the realistic, decorative, Victorian style uniquely associated with Baltimore.[12] By virtue of its being connected to Mary Evans through the "Notebooks," this block's style, a style which weaves through the Baltimore Album Quilts, has come increasingly to be thought of as Mary Evans's style.

If made during the heydey of the Baltimore Album Quilts, that City Springs block would have been begun one hundred or so years before being brought to Dr. Dunton. We won't ever know in detail what phrasing Mr. Bramble used to attribute this work to his great-aunt. But the passing of some one hundred years, one suspects, might cloud the Evanses', or any family's, recollection of exactly what Great-Aunt Mary's role in that block had been. Did Mary Evans design the elegant City Springs block herself? Or did she cut it out of fabric from someone else's design? Was her own work in this block at all, or had someone else cut and basted the motifs for Mary Evans to finish?[13]

One of the six accompanying blocks portrays a cleric and is labeled "John W. Hall," whom Dunton identifies in this article as the minister at the Caroline Street Methodist Church, just about three blocks from the portrayed City Springs. Both church and springs were in Mary's neighborhood.

Some of the other blocks in the set are already signed, though none "Mary Evans,"[14] and the needlework, in Dunton's words, varies in quality from "quite beautiful" to "rather crude." Might this have been a group-made presentation quilt with young Mary helping with the sewing? Or had these blocks come in from friends as contributions to Mary's own, never-finished, Album Quilt? Was she in fact a professional seamstress or simply the designated sewer who had been brought the basted center block to appliqué and the other blocks to set together when all were finished? In any one of these suggested roles, the block connected to her might have descended in her family as "the work of" Great-Aunt Mary. In the end, while the City Springs blocks does clearly reflect a design style, we don't know for sure whether this style is Mary Evans's or that of another. And if it is Mary Evans's, we don't know whether she originated the style or was one of a number of people working in that style.

This block was brought to Dunton with two completed quilts, both rather mundane square-patch variations. We are not told if they, too, were the work of Mr. Bramble's great-aunt, Mary Evans. What can safely be said is that, photographed in black and white, at least, they don't show the distinctive spark of an artist.

Katzenberg gives the birth/death dates for Mary Evans as 1829–1916 and cites the services in her book of Robert Barnes, genealogist. Dunton records what are presumably Evans Bramble's dates for Mary of 1830–1928. If Katzenberg is right, then Evans Bramble is wrong at least on this item in his facts about the block and its maker. One must also question why, if Mary were either an extraordinary needle artist or a prolific professional quiltmaker, her family had so little evidence about her quiltmaking activities. Mary Evans lived to be 87 years old by Katzenberg's dates or 98 years old by Evans Bramble's dates. By both reckonings she lived right into those early twentieth-century decades when Dunton himself was actively researching quilts. Yet the only evidence of quiltmaking activity to come out of all those years of adult life is an unfinished block said to have been begun when she was twenty.

While he records this block as made by "Miss Ford," William Dunton does not once suggest that she might be "the artist" whom he seeks as the maker of other Baltimore Album Quilts. In writing about this set of blocks he does reiterate his alternative theory that there may have been shops which sold patterns for these unusual designs. And Dunton's opinion of the possibility that Mary Evans may have been the artist in his theory? After having written about this "entertaining" set of blocks and Miss Ford in 1938, he left them and her out completely when, eight years later in 1946, he published his *magnum opus*, *Old Quilts*. Then again when, towards the end of his life, he compiled the files which "should go with the albums to the Baltimore Museum of Art . . . where [they] will be accessible to anyone who may be interested," he makes no mention of Mary Evans in all of the roughly two feet of alphabetized A to Z letter file boxes. He does, however, refer back once in those files to the City Springs block [with no attribution to Mary Evans]. In the manuscript section on "Naturalistic Appliqué," for his never-published *Quilt Dictionary*, he wrote: "There was also a large block made for a quilt which was never completed which showed a familiar sheltering, one of the City Springs. . . . Unfortunately during the absence of the owners, their house was broken into and this fine piece has been lost. Fortunately I had secured a photograph of it previously."

William Rush Dunton's works, both published and not, portray a fascinating, industrious, exceptionally bright man who corresponded with the major figures [all women] of the early-twentieth-century quilt world. He studied and documented in minute detail quilts from Maryland and nearby regions. As a founding father of occupational therapy, he "acquired a penchant for needlework and quilts, the peasant art of America." He believed quiltmaking was "a valuable means of restoring healthy thought" for "nervous ladies," and he self-published his book, *Old Quilts*, "in order to record some of the interesting bits of knowledge connected with some quilts and register the quilts, so to speak." Writing about the quilt dated 1850 and made for Dr. John P. MacKenzie in that ornate, Victorian style which we now identify with Baltimore, he conjectured: "It is unfortunate that the maker of such a masterpiece of needlecraft should be unknown. . . . Evidently the woman was an artist as is shown by her sense of form and color and probably in a later period would have been a painter. I have a theory which cannot be proved but which seems plausible to me, and that is, that she made her living by making quilts." Manifesting that *he* was still looking for that "artist," despite having been brought "the work of Mary Evans" some eight years earlier, he immediately follows the 1946 presentation of his theory with an open invitation for help: "It is hoped that old letters or other records will give information as to the name and personality of this wonderful needlewoman."[15] Further on he continued "I am of the opinion that these designs were probably sold at shops or that they were the work of one woman who practiced quiltmaking as a profession."[16]

In 1974, almost thirty years after the publication of *Old Quilts*, the Orlofskys wrote that "enterprising seamstresses may have supplied quilt block patterns much as needlepoint experts today. It is also believed that a professional needlewoman living in Baltimore, Mary Evans Ford, may have produced a number of these beautiful Baltimore Album quilts, . . . and as many as twenty-six."[17]

Seven years later in the Baltimore Musuem of Art's catalog to the 1980–1982 traveling exhibition, *Baltimore Album Quilts*, Dena

Katzenberg again presented the theory of Mary Evans's role in the Baltimore Album Quilts.

> An unfinished quilt block, one of a set of seven with pencil lines, and basted appliques, was brought to the attention of the quilt expert, Dr. William Dunton, by Arthur Evans Bramble. Bramble informed Dr. Dunton that the blocks were the work of his great-aunt, Mary Evans.... This piece established some of the hallmarks of Mary Evan's works: triple bowknots, prominent white roses, figures with inked features, the use of rainbow fabrics to indicate contour, a sure sense of formal design, and compositional skill. Such careful elegant work on so many quilts leads to the conclusion that a professional quiltmaker was at work. The author has identified over a dozen quilts which she considers to be the sole work of Mary Evans, and numerous individual blocks on other quilts.[18]

Katzenberg herself, later in her book is quite tentative about Mary Evan's possible authorship, as when she wrote of catalog quilt #14, "There is some reason to believe that the artist of the most proficient work on the Baltimore Album quilts can be identified as Mary Evans."[19] Ms. Katzenberg's research has unearthed a rich trove of information pertinent to Baltimore Album Quilts, but on the attribution to Mary Evans it seems not to be conclusive.

In 1983, my first book on these quilts, *Spoken Without a Word* was published.[20] It mentions the Mary Evans hypothesis as a subject treated in *Baltimore Album Quilts* by Dena Katzenberg, but concentrates on the thesis that these Album Quilts reflect Victorian use of symbols. In 1987, Schnuppe Von Gwinner's book, *The History of the Patchwork Quilt*, was published. In the chapter titled "Friendship and Album Quilts," it states: "Mary Evans and Achsa [sic] Godwin [sic] Wilkins of Baltimore were so talented and famous that they sewed whole album quilts and also individual blocks for others commercially."[21] This statement is not footnoted. Dunton is not listed in the bibliography but Katzenberg's *Baltimore Album Quilts* is included. *Baltimore Album Quilts* cites Dunton's *Old Quilts* for four out of six of Katzenberg's notes on Achsah Goodwin Wilkins (1775–1854), including the quote referring to her quiltmaking activity.

Also in 1987, the book *Hearts and Hands* included a statement of Mary Evans's role in these quilts:

> We now know from the meticulous research of Dena Katzenberg that many Baltimore album quilts were made with some or all of the blocks designed by professional quiltmaker Mary Evans. . . . The entrance of a professional like Baltimore resident Mary Evans into quiltmaking was a new departure. . . . Mary Evans's procedure [was] . . . supplying prefabricated blocks for which she received payment (and also . . . signing those blocks in a standardized script with their donors' names).[22]

By 1987, had new evidence turned up to confirm these conclusions? The footnote to the above quotation refers the reader back to the pages in *Baltimore Album Quilts* from which we have already quoted.[23] Yet it is these subtle shifts of *theory into fact* which may have set the tone for the confident attribution in January 1989 of Baltimore Album Style Quilts to Mary Evans. An evolution from hypothesis to postulate in the marketplace, parallel to that in the scholarship, is manifested by the repetition of the same set of three paragraphs describing Mary Evans's work being repeated in three consecutive Sotheby catalogs for three different Album Quilts. Sotheby's credits Julie Silber, co-author of *Hearts and Hands*, and Linda Ann Reuther for those paragraphs. Those excerpts reflect that book's confident view of Mary Evans's role in the authorship of Baltimore Album Quilts. The actual attributions for these three quilts and their publication sequence, are as follows: sale #5680, lot #1463 (January 1988), "Probably Mary Evans; sale #5755, lot #143 (October, 1988) no specific attribution is given in the notation "Variously signed," but the bulk of this quilt's description consists of discussion of Mary Evans; and, finally, for sale #5810, lot #1106 (Janary, 1989) the stated authorship is "attributed to Mary Evans."

Attribution to Mary Evans became markedly less ambiguous in the early winter of 1989, following a slower quilt market in the fall of 1988. "Quiet Time for Quilts, Caused by discriminating buyers who will settle only for the best," pronounced the title of an article by Frank Donegan in *Americana* magazine that year. He quoted Nancy Druckman, Sotheby's folk-art specialist as saying, "We're finding out that these [Baltimore Album Quilts] may not be as rare as we thought. A couple of $100,000 prices show you just how unrare something is."[24] Perhaps the irony of the story is that to this day the record high-selling quilt, a Baltimore Album Quilt signed by Sarah Pool and Mary J. Pool, sold by Sotheby's in January 1987, was not attributed to Mary Evans. Her name was not even mentioned in the catalog description although, by January 1989 standards, much of that quilt could have been attributed to her hand. The majority of its blocks are in the ornate, highly realistic, Victorian style associated with her name.

The increasing confidence of Mary Evans attributions for two of the three quilts offered for sale on January 21, 1989 of this year has left a paper trail. From the 1988 publication of E.P. Dutton's *Quilt Engagement Calendar 1989* to January, 1989, the wording changed on the attribution of the Gorsuch Baltimore Album Quilt: "Many blocks . . . may confidently be attributed to the hand of Mary Evans[25] became "Baltimore Album Quilt, made by the master American Quiltmaker, Mary Evans, circa 1845, for Eleanor [sic] Gorsuch, Baltimore County, Maryland."[26]

Similarly with the Updegraf Album Quilt offered by Christie's, the attribution to Mary Evans had also metamorphosed, though a bit more slowly. In the *Quilt Engagement Calendar 1984*, a description credited to Thomas K. Woodard concerning the Updegraf quilt's attribution reads, "It is quite probable that the quilt is the work of Mary Evans." Some five years later, in *The New York Times*, Rita Reif wrote: "An 1850 Baltimore Album Quilt by Mary Evans, the master quilt maker who created pieced coverlets with patriotic and nostalgic references between 1840 and 1860 is to be auctioned at Christie's."[27] Her article continues, "'She was the first professional quilt maker,' said Jan Wurtzburger, a Christie's folk-art specialist. [Can one assert that anyone was the *first professional quiltmaker*? We have evidence of bed quilts going back to the fourteenth century in Sicily—and has not the profession of seamstress in all its specializations been permitted to women for centuries?] 'This quilt has all the special hallmarks of her style—the triple bow knot, reticulated baskets, white appliquéd roses, intricate stitching and a careful and deliberate selection of the squares.'" Note that there is reference here to Mary Evan's intricate stitching and reticulated baskets though neither appear in the City Springs block.

Based on my own experience in examining needlework closely, I'd say that the three quilts attributed to Mary Evans and offered for sale in New York that January Saturday contained work by at least three different women. What is the same in all three quilts is the dominant pattern style: ornate, realistic, decorative, Victorian. But one style does not mean just one maker. What of the evidence from quilts done in the classic Baltimore Album style today? Some are as breath-taking in the mimicked fabric use and refined needlework as the vintage quilts they replicate. What, beyond age and period fabric, would distinguish these similarly styled quilts from the originals? Would we always be able to assess whether one person or more than one made a quilt of a uniform style? Again, the present aids our understanding of the past. In the March 1989 issue of *Country Living* magazine, Mary Roby reviewed the replica of the Metropolitan's Baltimore Album Quilt, ca. 1849, attributed in *Baltimore Album Quilts* to Mary Evans.[28] "It took a year for 30 quilters to complete . . . the quilt's top; . . . [more than] six women completed the quilting in five months." And what was the quality of the work having been done by so many people? "Meticulous uniform quality," the article concludes.

To set forth the pivotal differences in style and needlework among the three "Mary Evans" quilts offered for sale on that January Saturday would require an entire chapter. In short, the quilting of the Sotheby quilt has fewer stitches per inch than the Gorsuch quilt, and both quilts have at least one discolored block suggesting a different foundation fabric or a different age than the surrounding blocks. All three quilts have certain motifs in common. Cornucopiae, for example, are found in each, but the blocks differ significantly from quilt to quilt in those elements of style which might separate one maker from another. These elements include fabric use and ink embellishments, how much of the block is filled and in what shape, and how compact the bouquets are, and how much white space shows. How are we to know if Mary Evans made some or all of the blocks in any one of these three quilts?

Katzenberg concludes "Such careful elegant work on so many quilts leads to the conclusion that a professional quiltmaker was at work." Yet it is just that "conclusion" that has raised questions among scholars and quiltmakers. That Mary Evans made so many Album Quilts from start to finish just isn't consistent with what contemporary quiltmakers are learning about them. Many of us are making quilts in the classic Baltimore Album style, reproducing classic patterns or designing our own in this style, and keeping track of the hours we spend. I recorded about fifty sewing hours for an ornate Victorian style block like "Silhouette Wreath,"[29] and a bit less for the simpler "Ruched Rose Lyre." Professional quiltmaker Donna Collins, the speediest appliqué artist I know, reproduced the classic Baltimore Album Quilt block portrait of a Maryland Manor House[30] in about forty sewing hours, while Cathy Berry reported up to sixty hours to appliqué an intricate block such as "Red Woven Basket of Flowers."[31]

One professional quiltmaker, Sylvia Pickell, kept a meticulous log of the hours it took her to make "Immigrant Influences: Album of Heritage."[32] She spent 896 hours on handwork plus 200 hours on design, research, and drawing. Thus 1,096 hours went into making a quilt of 72 inches square, which is a bit less than half the square footage of the Baltimore Museum of Art's classic Baltimore Bride Quilt (104 inches x 104 inches) inscribed "To Miss Elizabeth Sliver" and attributed in the Baltimore Museum catalog to Mary Evans. Sylvia Pickell has demonstrated that a professional seamstress needs a year or more of forty-hour weeks to make one classic Baltimore Album Quilt of about 104 inches square. Therefore, a single individual (even one a bit faster than Sylvia) might conceivably create one quilt in the best of this style per year. Yet the equivalent of well over a dozen quilts by now have been popularly attributed to one woman, Mary Evans, in roughly a six-year period (1846–1852). Even presuming that one such quilt could be produced in a year, to produce six such masterpiece quilts in six years might be compared with writing six doctoral dissertations in six years in terms of the sheer intensity of creative effort involved.

Thus, while we cannot prove that Mary Evans made a given quilt, we can prove that one quiltmaker alone could not have made even the "more than a dozen" Baltimore Album Quilts attributed to her by Dena Katzenberg in roughly a six-year period. The important point is that if quilts aspire to art, then we need also to strive for the standards of authentication required in fine arts. No one would spend upwards of six figures on a painting by a famous artist without careful authentication. Yet comparably priced quilts have been sold on the most casual of assertions that they are made by Mary Evans with little or no documentation.

Baltimore Album Quilts deserve to be treated with as much respect as famous paintings. This respect requires reserving judgement in the absence of positive proof. Increasingly, cautious scholars, for example, are careful not to call a quilt a Baltimore Album Quilt unless "Baltimore" is inscribed on it or unless its provenance from that city or county is documentable. If these proofs are lacking in a quilt that seems in all other respects to fill the bill, they call it a "Baltimore-style Album Quilt." We need this kind of responsible standard in both scholarship and in the marketplace.

At least four equally ornate and complex Baltimore Album Quilts are supposed to have been made in about a two-year period from 1849–1850. These are the Metropolitan's Baltimore Album Quilt, recorded in *Baltimore Album Quilts* as "ca 1849;" the Baltimore Museum of Art's Album Quilt inscribed "To Miss Elizabeth Sliver" and "Baltimore, 1849;" the Baltimore Album Quilt inscribed to Dr. John P. Mackenzie and dated "February, 1850;"[33] and Christie's Updegraf family quilt dated 1850. All four are attributed to Mary Evans. The first three attributions are by Dena Katzenberg, the last, by Christie's. Could Mary Evans, or any one person have made these four quilts in so little time?

The most eloquent effort to fix Mary Evans's authorship to specific quilts is *Baltimore Album Quilts* by Dena Katzenberg. The argument there, however, is all circumstantial. The most potentially concrete evidence proposed is that "One signature of a Mary Evans Ford has been discovered on a 1909 application for admittance to the Aged Women's Home. Analysis of that handwriting suggests that it could have belonged to the person credited with almost half of the finest inscriptions on the quilts."[34]

I conferred with the personnel in the Documents Laboratory of the Federal Bureau of Investigation to find out if it was possible to ascertain if the signatures, written some sixty years apart, could have been done by the same hand. The question posed was: Could the classic Album Quilt inscriptions substantiate Mary Evans Ford's authorship? "Who knows?" one handwriting expert summed up. "You're never going to get a positive identification. I don't know anyone who would even give a leaning under these circumstances." One expert said, "When we do handwriting comparisons we don't like to deal with writing that is over five years apart."[35]

To sum up, "The Dog that Didn't Bark," convinced me that the

Mary Evans attribution in its present form was questionable. Dunton, of all people, was closest to Evans Bramble's attribution of the basted City Springs block to his Great-Aunt Mary. Whatever conversation passed between Dr. Dunton and Mr. Bramble, Dunton found that set of blocks "entertaining" but seemingly nothing more. The fact that that dog didn't bark when it should have for Dr. Dunton, served for me, as in Arthur Conan Doyle's detective story of the same name, as pivotal evidence.

The fact may remain, however, that theories about who made these quilts "cannot be proved" as Dr. Dunton wrote almost half a century ago. No matter who made the classic Baltimore Album Quilts, they are nonetheless national treasures. These heirlooms bind us to our past, give us continuity in the present, and offer us hope for the future. We may not ever be able to afix specific names with certainty to these quilts' design and manufacture. We can learn more about them, though, and in the process learn more about our culture and our past. By so doing we can help attain for these quilts, the work of so many earnest hands, their due regard.

Acknowledgments

This paper would not have been possible without help from the following people and institutions, acknowledged here with gratitude: Anita Jones, The Baltimore Museum of Art; Joel and Kate Kopp, America Hurrah Antiques, NYC; Sotheby's, and Christie's; Thomas K. Woodard, Thomas K. Woodard Quilts and Antiques; Frank J. Miele, Hirschl & Adler Folk, NYC; authors Patsy Orlofsky and Elaine Hedges; Katherine Campbell, for genealogical research; Mary Sue Hannan, Janet Sheridan, and Suzanne Carlson, the American Physical Therapy Association, for research assistance related to Dr. Dunton; Bill Carter and Documents Laboratory personnel, The Federal Bureau of Investigation; Erica Weeder, Japan Society Gallery, Meredith Schroeder and Marty Bowne, The American Quilter's Society for urging that this research be shared; Lee Porter, Laurel Horton, and the American Quilt Study Group for offering this paper a forum; and the contemporary quilters whose work and insights are shared here.

Notes and References

1. Rita Reif, "Auctions," *The New York Times* (January 13, 1989).
2. Pat Ferraro, Elaine Hedges, and Julie Silber, *Hearts and Hands: The Influence of Women & Quilts on American Society* (San Francisco, CA: Quilt Digest Press, 1987), 36.
3. "The Market," *Art and Antiques* (January 1989): 46.
4. *Sotheby's Catalog* (Sale # 5680): lot # 1463.
5. *National Antiques Review* (February 1972): 21.
6. Christie's Auction House, Sotheby's Auction House, and the annual New York Winter Antiques Show at the New York Armory, were three major antiques sales held the same January 1989 weekend.
7. *Sotheby's Catalog* (Sale #5810): lot #1106.
8. "The William Rush Dunton, Jr. Notebooks," uncatalogued collection, Baltimore Museum of Art.
9. Patsy and Myron Orlofsky, *Quilts in America* (New York: McGraw-Hill, 1974).
10. Marilyn Bordes, *12 Great Quilts from the American Wing* (New York: Metropolitan Museum of Art, 1974).
11. "Dunton Notebooks." Album VIII, 128. The text of the seven-page manuscript, dated 1938, follows:

> Back around 1850 there seems to have been a fashion of making quilts of an unusual character for presentation to some favored man or woman, often a clergyman. It was natural for the ladies of the congregation to show their regard by making a quilt to commemorate his incumbency.
>
> Among the quilts which I have met which are associated with churches or are of this presentation type perhaps the most entertaining is not a quilt but merely the makings as the various blocks have not been joined. One of these was made by Mary Evans Ford (1830–1928) when she was twenty years old, or in 1850, a member of the Caroline Street Methodist Church, not far from City Springs Square, Pratt and Eden Streets, Baltimore, Maryland. This was once a good residence section as is proved by the [blank] room in the American Wing of the Metropolitan Museum of New York, but is now a settlement of rather low class foreigners and there are few remnants of past grandeur now existing. Before this invasion began the house in which Miss ["Evans" crossed out] Ford lived was acquired by the church to be used as the parsonage.
>
> Miss Ford evidently had an attachment to the neighborhood for what was evidently intended to be the large central block of the quilt has in its centre a view of the park with the pavilion which covered the spring or "fountain," done in shaded browns which gives a high light effect to the suppporting pillars and also to the trunks of the trees which flank

it. The foliage of these is in various shades of green and blue. To the right a woman in a blue dress bears a brown pail on her head. To the left a very blonde lady is sitting on a bench beside a brown clad man. In front is a white rail fence with a brown and tan gate. Between the pillars of the pavilion pencil lines indicate tree trunks and a distant fence. This central scene is surrounded with a wreath of flowers with triple red bows above and below and triple lavender bows to right and left. In each corner are sprays of flowers. In the upper left is a rose of white mousseline, leaves of three shades of green and a brown stem. In the upper right corner are three brown and yellow pansies with leaves of two shades of green. In the lower right corner is a pink and red rose, two red and pink rosebuds, leaves of three shades of green and a brown stem. In the lower left corner are three blue flowers with yellow centres, presumably morning glories, with leaves of shades of green. The wreath effect is formed of the above mentioned bows with festoons of flowers between them. These show great variety including white mousseline and red roses, pansies, primroses and other flowers. The maker was an artist with a wonderful flair for color harmony and of the value of light and shadow so that her spective is exceptionally well handled. The piece is unfinished as all pieces to be appliquéd are basted on the white ground but the effect is quite beautiful. The muslin is 72 threads to the inch.

Accompanying this which was to have been the centre of an album quilt were six eighteen inch blocks some of which are signed. The most striking is that depicting the minister which is unsigned. At the bottom a flat shaded brown vase with a broad base from which extend on each side a curving spray of mixed flowers, white mousseline and red roses, tulips, pansies, moss rose buds with inked hairs and other flowers. Between these sprays stands the figure of the minister with black coat, brown pants, and black shoes. His white vest shows slightly and this, his shirt, collar and tie are indicated by inking. His head and face are partly inked and partly painted. The collar of his coat is broad and is appliquéd separately. His right arm extends down and the painted hand is holding a red edged open book marked "Hymns." His left hand (painted) rests on a tan and yellow book marked "Bible" which is on a red table. Above his head is an inked eagle with a scroll on which is "John W. Hall."

Dunton then goes on to describe the remaining blocks in the set: One with "quite a conglomeration of symbols [some he describes are shared by both Odd Fellows and Masons] and the name, "Nathaniel Lee" inscribed thereon; a "horn" (cornucopia) of "rather ungraceful" flowers and leaves, a heart of "angular leaves" outlined inside and out with a row of quarter-inch berries, and a cutwork square with a "a coarse red rose" on each side and parallel strips of small hexagons intertwined by rosevine. He concludes with subsequent history concerning the City Springs Square and its neighborhood in Baltimore.

12. While the Baltimore Album Quilts have multiple recognizably realistic representational blocks (buildings, flowers, birds, baskets, etc.), the style attributed to Mary Evans is more realistic even than they. In particular, this realism is conveyed through fine, artistic drafting of these objects, and through skillful use of printed fabrics to depict a realistic botanical or zoological or architectural detail.

13. Dunton himself long investigated questions raised by the set of seven blocks, as he did so many subjects touched upon by these quilts. His 1938 description of the seven blocks reflects research into the demographics of the City Springs area and the evolution of the Baltimore water system. Two years later, the 1940 letter quoted in Note #14, above, shows that Dunton was still researching the identity of John W. Hall whose name and whose portrait, apparently, appear in one of these seven blocks. Page seven of this Album VIII article gives us yet another clue about John Hall: "It is known that he assisted at laying the cornerstone of Grace Church." Early histories of Baltimore repeatedly note the laying of various cornerstones in the first half of the nineteenth century as "presided over by the Masons" and attended by "Masonic ritual." Both this reference and the notation of Masonic and Odd Fellow symbols in one block of this same set of blocks raise the question of how these blocks, and the Baltimore Album Quilts as a genre, may relate to fraternal orders. There is some reason to believe that pursuit of this question by scholars may shed more light on who was working in the style attributed in *Baltimore Album Quilts* to Mary Evans, and why there are so many blocks in that style in a short period of time. For more on this subject, see *Baltimore Beauties and Beyond, Studies in Classic Album Quilt Applique, Volume I – Pattern Companion* (Lafayette, CA: C & T, 1990).

14. Dunton notes no signature on the basted Springs block. However, after describing it in detail, he writes "Accompanying this which was to have been the centre of an album quilt were six eighteen blocks some of which are signed. He notes the signatures: "Mrs. Catherine A. Boyd," "Margaretta Stansbury," and "Mrs. Ann M. Bruscup."

15. William Rush Dunton, Jr., *Old Quilts*, (Catonsville, MD: privately printed, 1946), 41.

16. *Ibid.*, 118.

17. Orlofsky, 239.

18. Dena Katzenberg, *Baltimore Album Quilts* (Baltimore: The Baltimore Museum of Art, 1981), 61-62.

19. Ibid., 98.
20. Elly Sienkiewicz, *Spoken Without A Word, A Lexicon of Symbols with Twenty-Four Patterns from the Baltimore Album Quilts*, (Washington, D.C.: published by the author, 1983). The author's second book, *Baltimore Beauties and Beyond, Studies in Classic Album Quilt Appliqué, Vol. I* (Lafayette, CA: C & T, 1989), 26-27, 102-104, initiates the question of the Mary Evans attribution.
21. Schnuppe Von Gwinner, *The History of the Patchwork Quilt, Origins, Traditions and Symbols of a Textile Art*, (Munich: Keyser Book Publishing, 1987), 138.
22. Pat Ferraro, Elaine Hedges, Julie Silber, *Hearts and Hands: The Influence of Women & Quilts on American Society*, (San Francisco, Quilt Digest Press, 1987), 34-36.
23. *Baltimore Album Quilts*, 61-62.
24. Frank Donegan, "In the Marketplace: Quiet Time for Quilts," *Americana*, (Fall, 1988): 64.
25. *The Quilt Engagement Calendar 1989*, Cyril I. Nelson, comp. (New York: E.P. Dutton, 1988), illustrated May 7-13.
26. America Hurrah Antiques, full page ad, *Winter Antiques Show Catalogue* (January 1989): 45, in *The Magazine Antiques* (January 1989): unnumbered advertising page; and in *The Clarion* (Winter 1989): 7.
27. Rita Reif. "Auctions."
28. This replica was made by the East Bay Heritage Quilters. The estimates were provided by Adele Ingraham and Janet Shore.
29. *Baltimore Beauties, Volume I*, Colorplate # 24.
30. *Baltimore Beauties, Volume II*. (Lafayette, CA: C & T forthcoming late 1990).
31. *Baltimore Beauties, Volume I, Colorplate* © 35.
32. *Baltimore Beauties, Volume I*, Photo 31.
33. Dunton, 31-43; Roxa Wright, "Baltimore Friendship Quilt," *Woman's Day Magazine* (Fall 1965): 52, 53, 90.
34. *Baltimore Album Quilts*, 62. Further discussion of signatures is found on page 68-69.
35. Bill Carter of the Federal Bureau of Investigation Press Department, co-ordinator, with FBI Documents Laboratory personnel, interview by the author, Washington, D.C., February 28, 1989.

Signature Quilts:
Nineteenth-Century Trends

Barbara Brackman

Over the past twenty-five years, researchers in the fields of folklore, anthropology, and cultural geography have studied patterns in surviving nineteenth-century artifacts to determine the history and origins of American culture. By tracing the diffusion of innovations such as the banjo, gravestone motifs, and agricultural practices, inferences can be drawn about cultural influences. Backtracking along paths of diffusion has pinpointed four major points of origin for American cultural traditions: the New England (New York/Boston) area, the Midland Zone (the Valleys of the Susquehana and Delaware Rivers in eastern Pennsylvania and western New Jersey), The Chesapeake Bay region (near Baltimore), and the Southern Coast (from North Carolina to Georgia).[1]

Domestic architecture has been a popular subject for analysis ever since Fred B. Kniffen advocated using folk housing to reconstruct diffusion routes of material culture in 1965. He proposed that scholars identify and classify artifacts according to type and plot the types through time and space, geographical methods that allow interpretation of origins, dissemination routes, and the diffusion of a culture.[2] Using Kniffen's methods, Terry G. Jordan and Matti Kaups mapped dogtrot or open-passage folk housing throughout the United States and Europe, finding Finnish origins for this backwoods house rather than the purely British influence which had been suggested in the past.[3]

Folk housing, such as the dogtrot cabin, the shotgun house, or the Colonial Revival house, has several advantages for study. Buildings are diverse, yet classifiable according to form. They are durable, and they usually remain where they were built, giving later

---

Barbara Brackman, 500 Louisiana Street, Lawrence KS 66044.

observers the opportunity to map their occurrence and draw conclusions about settlement patterns and changes in style.

Quilts are similar in that they are diverse, yet classifiable. They are durable. Despite their apparent fragility thousands of nineteenth-century examples remain. But unlike buildings, quilts do not often endure in the spot where they were made. Their portability and practicality made quilts and bedding among the few household items that nineteenth-century migrants were encouraged to take with them on the road west.[4] The difficulty in determining exactly where an emigrant's quilt was made renders many of them useless for studying regional differences in quilt design or for studying patterns of migration and transmission of culture.

Signature quilts, however, are one type of quilt which can be analyzed using the methods Kniffen advocated for the study of folk housing. Signature quilts are group projects in which each block is sewn or signed by a different person. The finished quilt might be presented as a gift or kept by the organizer as a tangible reminder of friends and relatives.

The makers of signature quilts often recorded not only their names but their homes and the dates on the piece, so no matter where their current locations, the quilts reveal their origins in inked or embroidered inscriptions. Many of those without inscribed place names are accompanied by reliable family histories passed down with the quilts. Since a signature quilt contains records of several people, rather than of an individual, origins can often be corroborated using written records, such as censuses and church membership lists, which can pinpoint where and when the individuals lived as a community. In this paper I will examine the national distribution of the signature quilt style in the nineteenth century. Most researchers have focused on signature quilts from specific regions, primarily Baltimore, Maryland, and the Delaware River Valley. As a Kansan, I was interested in a wider view of the signature quilt. When I see an 1861 friendship quilt thought to be made in Lecompton, Kansas, or a Peabody, Kansas, sampler album that looks to be made in the 1850s, I want to know how accurate the Kansas attribution might be. Were Kansas settlers making signature quilts in the 1850s? How fast and how far did the signature quilt fashion spread?

While examining date-inscribed quilts as a means of developing guidelines for dating unsigned quilts,[5] I also analyzed signature quilts by plotting them across time and space to determine the source and transmission of the style. I collected data on quilts made anywhere in the United States. I used quilts I found pictured in current quilt literature and that of the recent past. I also used quilts I saw on exhibition and in museum and private collections. I relied on museum catalog cards when I could not see the quilts themselves, and I read some of the forms from three statewide quilt surveys (Quilts of Tennessee, the North Carolina Quilt Project, and the Kansas Quilt Project). At this point I have information on over 1,000 date-inscribed American quilts in a computerized file using DBase III. Of those, 227 were nineteenth-century signature quilts, upon which I have based this study.

I defined a signature quilt as a block-style quilt with more than one signature on its face. (Some had only two signatures.) I studied two types, the album in which each block is different, and the friendship quilt in which all the blocks are identical (although early examples often included a second design in the corners or center square.) As the terms "friendship quilt" and "album quilt" can be confusing, I will be more descriptive, calling the first a *sampler album*, the second a *single-pattern friendship* quilt. The designs in either may be piecework, embroidery, or applique. I omitted from the database fundraiser quilts, which also have more than one signature per block, and crazy quilts, as these styles were most popular after 1880 when magazines and other forms of popular culture began influencing what previously had been folk culture. In my database I included 121 sampler albums and 106 single-pattern friendship quilts.

Dates of Popularity

Those who have studied signature quilts are in general agreement about the dates of origin and peaks of fashion along the east coast. William Rush Dunton, the first to note the many signature quilts made in Baltimore, determined their heydey to be the years 1842 to 1853.[6] Dena Katzenberg, who studied Baltimore sampler albums, narrowed the dates of popularity in that city to 1846 to 1852.[7] Jessica Nicoll looked at signature quilts made in the Delaware River Valley areas of Delaware, Pennsylvania, and New Jersey and suggested a span of 1841 to 1855.[8] Jane Bentley Kolter described signature quilts made throughout the U.S. and concluded that 1840 was the starting point and 1870 the end of the style.[9] Linda Otto Lipsett characterized the span of signature friendship quilts as 1840 to 1875, with the 1840s and 1850s as the peak.[10]

The earliest signature quilt in the literature with a reliable date actually inscribed upon it is a single-pattern friendship quilt dated 1839-1843.[11] There are three signature quilts with blocks dated 1841, and twelve with blocks dated 1842, indicating that the idea of signing blocks for a group quilt caught on in the early 1840s. As the early examples usually contain blocks that span several years, it is difficult to determine if one type predates the other. However, four of the five quilts with blocks dated before 1842 are single-pattern friendship quilts, an indication that this style was initially more popular than the sampler album style.

The fad (and it does appear to be a fad with a sudden emergence and a sharp immediate rise followed by a trailing off of popularity) hit its peak in the mid-1840s and faded in the late 1850s. I found more dated examples of the sampler album than of the single-pattern friendship type; the sampler album type also maintained its initial popularity a few years longer. There were few examples of either type dated in the 1860s. The Civil War may have disrupted the practice during that decade, but a decline in both types is evident in 1853, eight years before the war began.

Kolter and Lipsett, who looked at quilts from the widest areas, indicated dates of 1870 and 1875, respectively, as the end of the album tradition.[12] However, a national overview of dated examples conflicts with this view. Rather than dying out, signature quilts enjoyed a revival in the 1880s and 1890s with a few changes. The single-pattern friendship quilt succeeded the sampler album as the more popular type in the last decades of the nineteenth century and into the twentieth. Sampler albums revived at the end of the century, but applique was no longer the most common technique. Album quiltmakers began to favor outline-embroidered blocks, a trend which continued into the twentieth century. The typical sampler album of 1930 might be a collection of floral blocks, em-

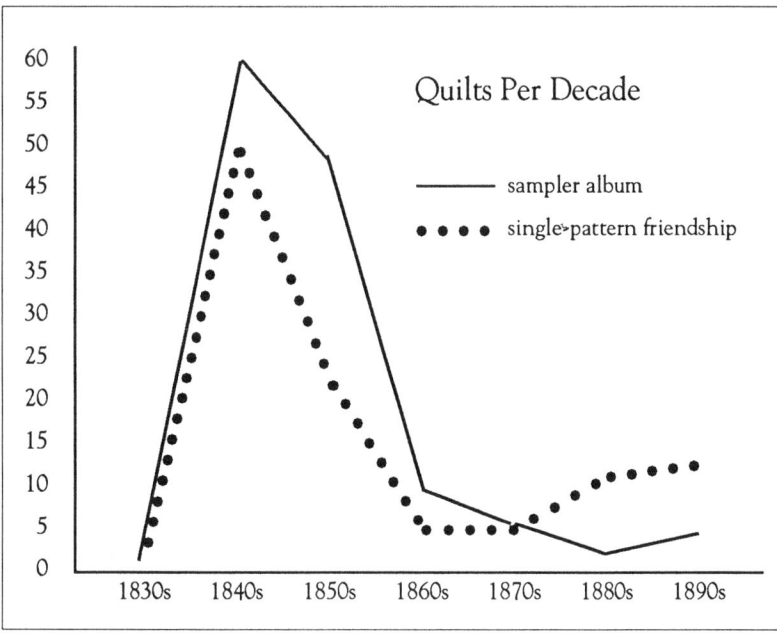

Figure 1. Incidence of Signature Quilts, 1840–1899.

broidered on pre-stamped squares sold by the Rainbow Quilt Company or Home Art Company.

I limited my study of signature blocks to the nineteenth century as I felt I lacked a national view of twentieth-century signature quilts. Few are pictured in books, collected by museums, or exhibited in galleries due to their visual qualities (currently unpopular with decorators and collectors), sources as kits and commercial patterns, and their relatively recent origins. My experience with twentieth-century signature quilts is limited to those I see in Kansas, primarily through the Kansas Quilt Project, but that observation indicates that embroidered sampler albums and pieced single-pattern friendship quilts were quite popular in Kansas in the 1920s and 1930s and this also may be true throughout the rest of the country.

In summary, examination of dated nineteenth-century examples corroborates information in the recent literature ascribing the origins of the signature quilt style to the early 1840s, followed by a sudden surge in popularity through the early 1850s, and a general decline in the 1860s and 1870s. It offers new evidence that the style revived in the 1880s and 1890s.

Geographic Patterns of Popularity

Kolter speculated that the fashion for signature quilts originated in Pennsylvania and Maryland and spread first to New York and Ohio, then to Virginia and North Carolina.[13] Nicoll described the source as the Delaware River Valley which runs along the Pennsylvania-New Jersey border.[14] A look at the earliest quilts (six quilts with blocks dated 1842) indicates that both are correct; the fashion seems to have originated in a wide area, from Morristown, New Jersey, south to Baltimore, generally along a line between the two largest cities of the era—New York and Baltimore. When the entire group of quilts dated before 1845 is mapped, the same area from Northern New Jersey along the Delaware River to the Chesapeake Bay is highlighted, with additional indications that the fashion had spread to western Maryland and central Virginia. Some geographic preference for type appears in the early years, as most of the single-pattern friendship quilts are grouped along the Delaware River and the early sampler albums range over a wider area from central Virginia north to Staten Island with the highest concentration in the Baltimore area.

During the next five-year period, 1845–1849, the signature style spread north to Maine, south to coastal South Carolina, and west to Ohio's Western Reserve. There is even one quilt in this period attributed to New Braunfels, Texas. However, most of the blocks made between 1845 and 1849 continued to spring from the Baltimore, Philadelphia, and New Jersey areas.

In the next five-year period, 1850–1854, the only significant geographical change is that Pennsylvania is no longer well-represented; the fad seems to have faded there first. By the period 1855–1859, the fashion had also waned in New Jersey and Baltimore. Apparently the urban trendsetters tired of the style while their rural sisters continued to organize signature quilts.

During the 1860s and 1870s, the few quilts made ranged over a wider area, as far west as Salt Lake City where the ladies of the

Female Relief Society made an appliqued sampler album in 1870, fifteen years after it had become *passe* in Baltimore.[15]

In the 1880s and 1890s, the single pattern friendship quilt began to increase in numbers, but little geographic clustering is evident. Quiltmakers from the Great Plains eastward made signature quilts. One area not represented, however, is the area where it all began. From New York City south to Baltimore, I found no dated examples in these decades.

Geographic clustering over the years indicated a continuing regional preference for type. The sampler albums were most popular early in the Baltimore and Philadelphia areas, while the single-pattern friendship quilts were preferred by quilters in the Delaware Valley of eastern Pennsylvania and western New Jersey. Sampler album quilts tended to cluster along the Baltimore-New York axis, while single-pattern friendship quilts were made in more scattered areas, especially central New York and New England, where few sampler albums were made.

Trends are also apparent in the distribution of the sampler album quilt. The fashion for signing quilt blocks was initially popular in and near Philadelphia. Three of the six sampler albums dated 1842 come from that city and its environs, and only one from Baltimore. They do not feature the complex applique patterns that we consider the hallmark of the sampler album. One of the six (from Philadelphia) is entirely pieced and another (from Lisbon, New Jersey) is all appliqued of cut-out chintz or *broderie perse*. The rest are a combination of intricately pieced blocks, cut-out chintz, and rather simple applique, with piecework the predominant technique. We do not begin to see the classic applique sampler we call a Baltimore Album quilt until 1845 or 1846. I surmise that the idea of a sampler began in the Philadelphia area and spread rapidly to Baltimore, where seamstresses developed the distinctive applique sampler that eclipsed the earlier sampler of elaborate pieced blocks, which might be referred to as the Philadelphia Album.

Most of us are familiar with the applique Baltimore Album look. It is important to note that these elaborate appliqued sampler albums were not exclusively from Baltimore, even in the early years, but were also made in Pennsylvania, Connecticut, Virginia, and other eastern seaboard states.

Figure 2. Sampler album quilt, made for Mary E. Mannakee (1827–?) in Montgomery County, Maryland. Inscribed 1850–1851. Collection of the Daughters of the American Revolution Museum, Washington, D.C. Gift of Mrs. Benjamin Catching.

In summary, the style began in the Midland and Chesapeake Bay zones and rather quickly diffused north and south along the Atlantic coast, and as far west as Ohio. As the fashion for signature quilts faded in the east after the Civil War, it appeared in the newly-settled western states.

Because mid-century signature quilts are found all over the United States today, one is inclined to believe they were made throughout the country. The data indicate that during the first twenty years of the style, a national view of the signature style is actually a regional view. Although there were twenty-eight states in the union in 1847, when the style was at its peak, signature quilts were most likely to be made in only half of them. The women who settled the western states in the 1840s and 1850s may have brought their signature quilts with them, but the idea of making them did not diffuse so rapidly.

The pattern of migration demonstrated by these figures should encourage a sense of skepticism in ascribing mid-western origins for mid-century signature quilts. A personal example: After looking at the data, I checked the 1860 and 1865 censuses for names of the alleged Lecompton settlers who made the quilt dated 1861 (the year of Kansas statehood) and found none of them. It was most likely made in the eastern United States and brought to Kansas at a later date.

Construction Trends as Clues to Date

The patterns of origin and diffusion can assist quilt historians in assigning geographical locations to signature quilts. Some details of construction can also be useful clues to date. Most sampler albums in the database had blocks of identical size, but some quiltmakers persisted with an older concept, a central design focus, obtained by including one large block in the center of a field of equally-sized blocks. Thirty per cent of the sampler albums dated between 1840 and 1844 included this central design focus, a format that faded over the years. Between 1845 and 1849, only eleven per cent featured larger blocks in the center. Not one sampler album dated in the 1850s had a central focus, an indicator that a larger block in the center of the quilt is a clue to a sampler album from the 1840s.

Observation also indicated that sampler album quilts and samplers made by individuals in the 1840s and 1850s can be characterized as orderly. After the Civil War we begin to see a hodge-podge of different block sizes arranged rather haphazardly. Thus a chaotic arrangement of different size blocks is an indication of a date after 1865.

Trends in Applique Patterns

I had projected that studying signature quilts would give me some insight into pattern development, especially the origins and diffusion of the traditional applique designs that developed at the same time as the sampler album. To track trends, I cut up photocopies of ninety-two sampler albums, dated from 1840 to 1876, and organized the hundreds of applique blocks into groups of similar patterns, such as fleurs-de-lis, bouquets, closed wreaths, and open wreaths. I sought to create an index useful in identifying the source of undated quilts, for example, an unsigned applique sampler found in Peabody, Kansas, by the Kansas Quilt Project.[16] I knew it was unlikely to be Kansas-made, but was it a Baltimore quilt? I could not match the eighteen blocks to the hundreds in the index. Although there are similar baskets or wreaths, an identical design or even a near match is rare. I am not optimistic that this sort of pattern index could help date or place a quilt beyond a general attribution of "1840–1860, probably east coast of the United States."

Through the pattern index I also attempted to support my thesis that the popularity of the sampler album style generated the applique designs that became popular for single-pattern quilts made by individuals. However, I found my sample too small to yield reliable conclusions. I did find that most of the standard applique designs appeared concurrently as single-maker, single-pattern quilts and as blocks in sampler albums. The Mexican Rose appears in single-pattern quilts dated 1849 and 1853 (two examples), and in sampler albums dated 1847, 1853, 1855 (two examples), and 1863. The Fleur-de-Lis appears in dozens of sampler albums made after 1844 and in single-pattern quilts dated 1846–1848, 1856, and 1859. However, I have too few dated examples of most patterns and the dates are too close to determine whether the design originated as a sampler album pattern or as a single-maker, single-pattern quilt. One exception is the Oak Leaf and Reel design, which was quite common in both types of signature quilts. There are single-pattern, single-maker quilts in this design dated 1818, 1829, and 1830. It is one of the few applique patterns that predates the signature style.

Most of the standard applique designs that appeared after 1840 seem to have originated in the Baltimore-Chesapeake Bay area. One exception is a symmetrical arrangement of hearts that seems to have developed in the New York-New Jersey region.[17] A few patterns that were very popular for single-pattern quilts by individuals, such as the Princess Feather and the Whig Rose, rarely appeared in album quilts. The complexity of these designs often dictates a large block (18 inches or more), which may have deterred quiltmakers from using them in the smaller blocks that generally made up signature quilts. However, equally complex designs were popular for album quilts, so some other factors may have influenced the categorization of some designs as more appropriate for single-pattern quilts by individual makers. The reverse is more commonly true. Many designs popular in the album quilts never became standard patterns. The broad range of applique patterns in the sampler albums of the mid-nineteenth century indicates that the makers were exploring the design possibilities of a new technique. Certain patterns caught on and spread around the country; others disappeared after a few years or one single block. These signature quilts were design workbooks as well as expressions of friendship.

Conclusion

This study indicates a definite regional origin for the signature quilt style, an origin in the Midland and Chesapeake regions that have generated many of the vernacular arts we define as American's folk culture. My work represents an adaption of geographic methodology using quilts as artifacts. As state and regional surveys of quilts add to our database we will have more opportunities to study quilts in their geographic contexts. Signature quilts from the Philadelphia region in the early 1840s may offer interesting contrast to the Baltimore-Chesapeake Bay quilts of the same years, and signature quilts from the South Carolina coast may show regional variations in the 1850s and 1860s. More information on quilts from the south (northern quilts are currently collected and pictured far more often than southern quilts) may give us additional insight into the diffusion of the signature style.

State and county quilt projects acquiring information about quilts which are reliably attributed to specific geographic origins can also use these methods with quilts other than signature quilts. By comparing types across regions we may soon be able to draw many new conclusions about the origins and diffusion of mid-nineteenth century pattern and style.

Notes and References

1. Wilbur Zelinsky, *The Cultural Geography of the United States* (Englewood Cliffs, NJ: Prentice Hall, 1973), 83; Henry Glassie, *Pattern in the Material Folk Culture of the Eastern United States* (Philadelphia: University of Pennsylvania Press, 1968), 35-36. Zelinsky lists three nuclear nodes for cultural dissemination: Southern New England, The Midland, and the Chesapeake Bay region. Glassie lists four.
2. Fred B. Kniffen, "Folk Housing: Key to Diffusion," in *Annals of the Association of American Geographers* 58 (1965): 549-77.
3. Terry G. Jordan and Matti Kaups, "Folk Architecture in Cultural and Ecological Context," in *The Geographical Review* 77, no. 1 (January 1987): 52-75.
4. Among the guidebooks that listed bedding as a top priority for pioneers are Rudolph B. Marcy, *The Prairie Traveler: A Hand-Book for Overland Expeditions* (New York: Harper, 1859), 40; and James Redpath and Richard Hinton, *Hand-book to Kansas Territory and the Rocky Mountains Gold Region* (New York: Colton, 1859), 30. Marcy suggested, "The bedding for each person should consist of two blankets, a comforter, and a pillow, and a gutta percha or painted canvas cloth to spread beneath the bed upon the ground and to contain it when rolled up for transportation."
5. Barbara Brackman, *Clues in the Calico: A Guide to Identifying and Dating Antique Quilts* (McLean, VA: EPM, 1989).
6. William Rush Dunton, *Old Quilts* (Catonsville, MD: privately printed, 1946), 175.
7. Dena S. Katzenberg, *Baltimore Album Quilts* (Baltimore: Baltimore Museum of Art, 1981), 14, 65.
8. Jessica F. Nicoll, *Quilted for Friends: Delaware Valley Signature Quilts, 1840-1855* (Winterthur, DE: Henry Francis Dupont Winterthur Museum, 1986), 5.
9. Jane Bentley Kolter, *Forget Me Not: A Gallery of Friendship and Album Quilts*, (Pittstown, NJ: Main Street Press, 1985), 9, 52.
10. Linda Otto Lipsett, *Remember Me: Women and their Friendship Quilts* (San Francisco: Quilt Digest Press, 1985), 19.
11. The example inscribed 1839-1843 is pictured in Kolter, plate 93. There are a few signature quilts in the literature with earlier dates that ap-

pear to be altered or of a commemorative nature, rather than the date the quilt was made. See the ELI quilt dated 1817 in Myron Orlofsky and Patsy Orlofsky, *Quilts in America* (New York: McGraw Hill, 1974), 235, and a quilt dated 1828–1891 in Mary Merriam and Suzanne C. Flynt, *Quilts* (Deerfield, CT: Pocumtuck Valley Memorial Association, 1985), 21. The fabrics, patterns and style in both appear to be far later than the inscribed dates.
12. Kolter, 52; Lipsett, 19.
13. Kolter, 10.
14. Nicoll, 7.
15. Quilt is pictured in Kate B. Carter, *Pioneer Quilts* (Salt Lake City: Daughters of Utah Pioneers, 1979), 71.
16. Kansas Quilt Project #Fa125.
17. An example of a single-pattern quilt in a variation of this design is pictured in Marguerite Ickis, *The Standard Book of Quilt Making and Collecting.* (New York: Greystone, 1949; reprinted by Dover, 1959), 47. She calls it "Traditional Geometric Design."

Early Influences of the Sewing Machine and Visible Machine Stitching on Nineteenth-Century Quilts

Suellen Meyer

When Isaac Merritt Singer turned his considerable talents toward perfecting the sewing machine, he was looking only for a way to get rich quick. He succeeded—and in the process, he transformed sewing from a tedious, time-consuming task into a mechanized one. Seamstresses saved considerable time: by hand, a man's shirt required fourteen and a half hours of sewing time, but by machine, only a little more than one hour. Making coats, dresses, nightclothes, underclothes, and children's clothes became merely a nuisance, not the overwhelming burden it had been. Quiltmakers devoted their newfound time to making more quilts, some of which they embellished with visible machine stitching, an indication of the pride they felt in their sewing machines.

Many inventors had tried to perfect a sewing machine, some working to reproduce the movement of the human hand, others to duplicate the stitch. In 1755, a London mechanic, Charles Weisenthal, patented a machine with a revolutionary eye-pointed needle, later to be the central feature of all sewing machines.[1] In 1834, Walter Hunt, a New York inventor, duplicated the stitch, not the movement of handsewing. His machine included a spool above the fabric and one below with a shuttle between; as the shuttle moved the threads, it locked them together, making a lockstitch—a grand improvement over the chainstitch which unraveled at any break.[2]

Some elements of Hunt's machine resurfaced in the machine later

---

Suellen Meyer, Professor of English, St. Louis Community College—Merrimack, 11333 Big Bend, St. Louis MO 63122.

developed by Elias Howe, a New England mechanic. Because Howe became too ill to work, his wife took in sewing to support the family. Howe saw firsthand the toll sewing took on her and became obsessed with inventing a sewing machine, finally patenting a practical one in 1846. Although an expert mechanic, Howe lacked merchandising savvy and proved unable to sell his machine. Meanwhile, other American inventors, among them Isaac Merritt Singer, were trying to invent a practical machine.

Singer had no interest in easing women's burdens. In fact, when a friend first suggested that he invent a sewing machine, Singer shouted, "You want to do away with the only thing that keeps women quiet—their sewing!" But once convinced that he could make a lot of money quickly, Singer improved on Howe's needle and shuttle, and in a flash of mechanical genius, combined the ten components that became standard on all sewing machines. Even today, machines include the lockstitch, an eye-pointed needle, a shuttle for the second thread, continuous thread from spools, a horizontal table, an overhanging arm, continuous feed, thread or tension controls that change the tautness of thread, a presser foot, and the ability to sew in a curving or straight line.[3]

In 1848, Howe returned from an unrewarding sales trip to England. In America, he learned that his wife was dying from consumption and that other men were selling sewing machines—machines suspiciously like his own invention.[4]

Howe and the sewing machine companies fought bitterly over patent rights in the design of different machines. Finally realizing that only the lawyers were getting rich, three companies—Singer, Wheeler and Wilson, and Grover and Baker—created the first patent pool, the Sewing Machine Combination. Each company contributed $15.00 for every machine sold; after expenses, they shared this money equally. To persuade Howe to join, the companies paid him $5.00 for each machine sold in addition to his share of the profits. Between 1856, the date of the Combination, and 1867, when his patent expired, Howe earned at least $2 million—without ever manufacturing a machine.[5]

Before the outbreak of the Civil War, sewing machine companies concentrated on selling factory models to manufacturers who could afford the high prices. In 1862, clothing manufacturers owned three-quarters of all machines.[6] The larger market, that of women at home, was waiting to be tapped. The Singer Company led the way with its lightweight Turtleback machine and its inventive marketing strategies. The company combatted two entrenched myths held by Victorian men: first, that women couldn't control machinery, and, second, that, freed from some of their arduous labors, women would go wild.

Although campaigns to disprove both these myths took place simultaneously, the Singer Company found it simpler to prove that women could in fact handle machines. Up to the mid-1800s, people believed that men had the intelligence and temperament for machines; women, those delicate creatures, could use tools (needles, brooms, washboards) but not machines. In order to counteract the public's notions about machinery, I. M. Singer and Company insisted that all demonstrations be conducted by young women. (They paid sales agents $6.00 a month extra if their *wives* could demonstrate the machines.)[7]

Other sewing machine companies imitated Singer's approach. Grover and Baker's St. Louis agent advertised that "A Lady will always be in attendance to exhibit the Machine and give instructions free."[8] Other brochures bragged that "it is so simple in its construction, so accurate and reliable in its execution, that even a child can manage it with success," a not-too-subtle suggestion that if children could control a machine, their mothers might also manage.[9] *Godey's Lady's Book* assured its readers that women could learn to operate sewing machines. The editor added that the machines would not only teach some science to the wives, but that "the boys under their charge, the men in miniature, would have their curiosity aroused in contact with the finest and most effective . . . machinery of modern times."[10]

Sewing machine companies soon won the war of ability. Convincing men that women would use their additional time wisely took longer. Most companies interpreted "wisely" as meaning women would devote more time to the needs of their families, particularly of their husbands. Singer's ads insisted that women would be more rested, more able to supervise the children, more capable of providing their husbands with comforts previously available only to the wealthy.[11]

Godey's also encouraged this view. In 1863, it devoted its frontispiece to two views of the sewing machine: The Old Sewing Machine

Figure 1. Trade card emphasizes that children can handle Singer's sewing machines. Collection of Annette and George Amann.

pictured a bare room, with a plainly dressed woman hunched over her work, sewing by candlelight, a mound of other sewing before her. The next month featured The New Sewing Machine—a lovely bright parlor, a woman instructing her elder daughter on the machine, a younger child sitting at her feet playing with her doll, an open magazine beside her.[12]

Women had to find the money to purchase machines—and they were not cheap. When introduced, sewing machines sold for $125, a steep price when the average annual family income was only $500.[13] In contemporary terms, the machine equalled a car—paid for in cash, with no chance of credit. A farmwoman, Elizabeth Welty, figured the family would have to thresh over 1,600 bushels of wheat for her to get a machine.[14] Even after the price fell, many families couldn't afford machines. *Godey's* encouraged groups of families to unite, each contributing a portion of the cost and each getting use of the machine for two and half days per month.[15]

Many women who owned machines did share them. Alceste Huntington wrote her mother that she "was so excited with the thought of the amount of sewing I had to do that I was awake at daylight. . . .

Figure 2. Frontispiece in *Godey's Lady's Book* shows a woman's weariness from sewing by hand.

Julia Gritten [a neighbor] is helping with her machine."[16] Talula Bottoms used her mother-in-law's hand-turned machine until 1895, when she bought her first pedal machine.[17] When Maria Wicker visited St. Louis, she learned to sew on a machine and proudly wrote her son, "Lou is making some clothes for Millie. . . . I have learned to run a Wheeler and Wilson machine that Mrs. Ronlet left in the house and am able to help considerably."[18]

In order to discourage sharing, Edward Clark, Singer's partner, offered a solution few families could resist. In 1856, he suggested that a family lease the machine (five dollars down, with the rest paid in

Figure 3. Contrasting frontispiece in *Godey's Lady's Book* shows the ease of sewing with a machine.

monthly installments of three to five dollars). Immediately, sales skyrocketed from 883 in 1855 to 2,564 in 1856. Singlehandedly, Clark created the installment plan, still used in many consumer sales.[19]

Amanda Slaughter, in a time-honored rural tradition, combined the installment plan with bartering. The peddler brought a machine to her Missouri farm home and offered to leave it for a few days. Amanda got it on Tuesday; on Wednesday, they came to terms — a total of $75 with a down payment of Rose, the cow valued at $35 and monthly payments of $5 until the remaining $40 was paid.[20]

In 1857, Edward Clark introduced the trade-in allowance. He

offered $50 for every old sewing machine of any make, promising to destroy them since they couldn't possibly match Singer's quality. Clark's move was brilliant marketing; he enticed owners of machines made by other companies to trade for Singer's machines, ensuring that these machines could not be sold on the second-hand market. At the same time, by giving customers a trade-in allowance even for old Singer machines, he encouraged brand loyalty. Singer's sales rose half again from 2,564 to 3,630 for that year.[21]

Machines sold first to women living near the manufactures—the Singer Company and Willcox and Gibbs in New York City; Clark and Baker in Orange, Massachusetts; Bodgett and Lerow in Boston; and Wheeler and Wilson in Watertown, Connecticut. Since most factories were in the Northeast, women there were most likely to have machines. In 1860, the Civil War brought a disruption of transportation and trade between the regions and delayed the widespread sale of sewing machines in the South.

Women, both North and South, sewed for their men in uniform, providing clothing, sheets, blankets, and quilts. In the industrial North women organized themselves into sewing groups and, using machines lent by merchants, sewed for the army, turning out 1,000 shirts in two days. By 1865, women had made 250,000 quilts and comforts for the Union soldiers, many of them probably pieced by machine.[22]

Southern seamstresses lucky enough to own machines used them heavily. Judith Brockenbrough McGuire of Alexandria, Virginia, confided to her diary, "Our soldiers must be equipped. Our parlor was the rendezvous for our neighborhood, and our sewing-machine was in requisition for weeks. Scissors and needles were plied by all."[23] Judith and her friends switched to handsewing when the blockade prevented the importation of factory-made thread. Homemade thread proved too uneven for machine use.[24] Because machine sewing required from two to five times as much thread as hand sewing, Southern women with limited access to thread were more likely to sew by hand. Northern soldiers searching Confederate homes seized guns and damaged sewing machines. After one party searched her home, Judith reported,

> I believe they took nothing but the rifle, and injured nothing but the sewing-machine. Perhaps they knew of the patriotic work of that same machine— how it had stitched up many a shirt and many a jacket for

our brave boys, and therefore did it wrong. But this silent agent for our country's weal shall not lie in ruins. When I get it again, it shall be repaired and shall
"Stitch, stitch, stitch,
Band, and gusset, and seam,"
for the comfort of our men, and it shall work all the more vigorously for the wrongs it has suffered.[25]

Deprived of the necessary thread and replacement parts, Southern women depended on the needle for their tasks.

Thus, Northern women developed their technical expertise and expanded their uses of the machine earlier than did Southern or Western women who did not have access to sewing machines. Once the war was over in 1865, the distribution of the sewing machine widened dramatically, as did women's experimentation with it.

Women began by learning to control the machine, a task more difficult than it appeared. Instruction in the sales-room or the card of directions enclosed with mail-order made the machine appear simple to operate. However, machine sewing required practice, as a California woman discovered in 1860:

> The next day my precious machine was unpacked, and following the printed directions, I succeeded in fixing the cotton and threading the needle, which was already properly set. It seemed so perfectly easy to work, as I had seen the man at the store operating upon it, that I spurned the idea of trying on a rag, and confidently put under the cloth-presser a leg of a pair of drawers for one of the children, that I had just cut out and basted. . . . [I] put my foot upon the treadle and started off. The wheel made a revolution forward, and then came back with great facility; my work moved the wrong way; the cotton became mixed up in a lamentable manner, and when I endeavored to pull the work into place, crack! went the needle. . . . Early on Monday morning I was again at work, and had the happiness of actually making stitches. To be sure they were in all directions, of various lengths, as I had pulled or held back the work, and their loose appearance was not very satisfactory to a neat seamstress as I profess to be. Still, there was no getting over the fact that they were actual stitches.[26]

Such time-consuming practice proved worthwhile. The machine not only stitched ordinary items quickly, but it also served as an important status symbol. So important was the machine that Worth of Paris, a major couterier, used the machine for the top-stitching on his fabulously expensive gowns which were otherwise entirely handsewn.

Seamstresses developed their expertise by sewing clothing on the machine. Next they eyed the inevitable bedding. The large families of the nineteenth century – and the servants who worked for them – needed many bedcovers. According to an 1883 issue of *Arthur's Home Magazine*, three-quarters of these covers were quilts.[27] If so, a sizable number must have been utility quilts, quickly made with inexpensive domestic cloth and the sewing machine.

Women probably made many machine-quilted, utility coverings. In doing so, they adapted the machine beyond the companies' imagination. Early ads promoting quilting attachments and touting machine quilting were aimed at tailors who bought hand-quilted fabric for linings of vests and coats. When cost-conscious factory owners replaced hand-quilted linings with machine-quilted fabric, women applied the idea to bedquilts which they quilted in squares, from one to four inches wide – much like the grid of the commercially-quilted lining materials.[28]

No doubt seamstresses found it difficult to control the three layers of top, batt, and lining while treadling the machine, for the working space was shallow, and the thread often broke. Once adept, however, some turned their attention to their fine quilts, where the visible stitch testified to their skill.

It is difficult to determine how many nineteenth-century quilts have visible machine stitching in the applique or quilting. Such quilts are much rarer than quilts which include machine piecing. Jonathan Holstein asserts that while machines were seldom used for applique or quilting, they were commonly employed for piecing. He reports that about half of the quilts he has seen which date after the 1860s are machine pieced and that the edges of both applique and pieced quilts are commonly finished by machine.[29] While machine-stitched bindings have been accepted, collectors and dealers have devalued other visible machine stitching, so these examples tend not to be displayed for sale or in shows. Still, such quilts exist in private family collections and in some museum collections. Perhaps as many as ten per cent of all quilts during the period from 1865 to 1900 in some areas bear some machine applique or quilting.

Sometimes machine quilting appears as a grid over the surface of a full-size quilt, or individual blocks may be quilted and then joined in the quilt-as-you-go manner. Robert Cargo owns a curious small piece, just twenty inches square, with a bright red-and-green Feathered Star in the center.[30] Using the machine, the quilter has quilted around each piece making up the star, has quilted the ground in close parallel rows, and has quilted the center in small squares. This unusual piece from the fourth quarter of the nineteenth century may have been designed as an entry for a fair or to demonstrate the maker's proficiency with her sewing machine.

Women across the country tried their hands at machine quilting. Some sewing machine companies provided quilted pieces for inspiration. In 1859, Grover and Baker entered quilting in the sewing-machine work category at the Sacramento, California fair. For a time in the late 1800s, Iowa fairs gave a premium for machine quilting. These may have been specimens (perhaps like Robert Cargo's piece), not quilts, but in 1882, Mrs. M. E. Shaffer of Ashew, Iowa, won two dollars for her machine-quilted white quilt.[31] Many quiltmakers mixed hand quilting and machine quilting on the same quilt. In 1889, Mathursa Jane Craft received a sewing machine for Christmas. As she finished a Pine Tree quilt for her daughter Lucrita, she switched from her quilting needle to her sewing machine, quilting the border by machine and finishing with a flourish in one corner, "New Year's Eve 1889/Crita."[32]

Very few quiltmakers used the machine for extravagant quilting. One who did created an amazing full-size, white-on-white quilt, the entire surface closely quilted by machine. The center of the quilt features two doves perched in a branch. They sit in a circle in which the free spaces have been filled in with six five-pointed stars. A circle of scrolls surrounds this center design. Outside the scrolls the maker has quilted a variety of designs including a cherub playing a triangle, a dove with a ribbon in its mouth, and a large public building with a flat roof and many arched windows. Below the building the quiltmaker has stitched.

Singer Machine Work
By M J Foster   Ottawa Illinois

Other designs on the quilt include a large three-masted sailing ship with square sails and an American flag at the stern, two spread eagles holding in their beaks American flags with thirteen stars, another public building smaller than the first, and another ship with a triangle sail at its back. As if this *tour de force* were not enough, all free spaces on the surface have been stitched in crossed diagonals, with foilage patterns, or with scrolls so that the entire quilt is covered with stitchery.[33] Although the details of M.J. Foster's life are unknown, the quiltmaker was clearly a virtuoso with Mr. Singer's machine.

By the end of the century, machine quilting had become *declasse* in fashionable circles. Rural readers still asked the editors of publications such as *Comfort* for instructions for machine quilting. In 1906, the editors obliged with these directions: "To quilt on the machine do one block at a time, making it so much easier to handle. You can have a gauge so that all will be uniform, the lining is put on afterwards, only needing some thin material for the lining of each block to quilt through."[34] More fashion-conscious magazines exhorted women to return to hand quilting even if they had to seek out older quilters. In 1894, after describing the way to piece a quilt, Sybil Lanigan suggested a quilting bee as "the merriest and quickest way of finishing the quilt," assuring the reader that "the worst way of all is to use a sewing machine for the purpose, and the best is to find some skillful, old-fashioned sewing woman."[35]

Although most late-nineteenth-century quiltmakers preferred to finish thier quilts with handquilting, many used their machines to construct the tops. Some used their sewing machines to applique since this allowed them to show off both their machines and their skill. Most sewers found it more difficult to handle curves and points with the machine than by hand. Some women, like an anonymous slave in New Madrid, Missouri, used the machine for the entire top: Instructed to make a quilt for her mistress's birthday, she surprised her master by machine appliqueing large, showy flowers.[36]

In the nineteenth century, certain applique designs such as Tulip, Princess Feather, and Cockscomb and Currant became recognized as show quilts, that is, quilts made for the pleasure of their artistry rather than for use. Some women used their sewing machines to create similar appliqued and quilted showpieces. About 1870, Jane Richey Morelock of Bradley County, Tennessee, designed an extravagant Cockscomb and Currant quilt constructed of four large blocks. The design included flowers, leaves, buds, vines, and grapes.

Jane used both the sewing machine and the hand-held needle to applique the intricate design.[37] We don't know whether she began with the machine and finished with the needle or vice versa. However, her willingness to use the sewing machine to applique part of her Cockscombs and Currant design suggests her pride both in her dexterity with the machine and also in the machine itself.

Like Jane Richey Morelock, Harriet Powers used both the needle and the machine to applique her Bible quilts now housed in the Smithsonian Institution and the Museum of Fine Arts in Boston. She used the machine for all the figures—Adam and Eve, the serpent, animals of all kinds, and the angels—while she appliqued the folded stars by hand. This mixture of hand and machine sewing appears repeatedly in quilts in the fourth quarter of the nineteenth century. Toward the end of the century many quiltmakers pieced baskets by hand and appliqued the handles by machine, combining their tools to complete one quilt. Quiltmakers could applique the handles more quickly by machine than by hand, but perhaps more importantly, this visible machine stitch reflected their pride in their machines.

Like many late-nineteenth-century quiltmakers, Mary Parks Lawrence of Logan County, Kentucky, experimented with the power of the machine. At the age of sixteen she was an accomplished seamstress, responsible for the family sewing. Her father gave her a machine when she promised to sew all the family's coats, and Mary used it as well in her 1870 Cherry Basket quilt. Using a needle, she hand-appliqued the orange and red flowers and baskets; using the machine, she applied the green basket handles and leaves and stems. She hand-quilted exquisite feather wreaths and running feathers, filling in the background with one-quarter-inch diagonal lines. Still eager to try out her machine, she reserved the narrow white borders for machine quilting.[38] This masterpiece reflected both her traditional training (most girls learned to sew before they started school) and her acquisition of new techniques.

Yet another quiltmaker, Narcissa Black, a skilled professional seamstress in McNairy County, Tennessee, used both the hand-held needle and the sewing machine. In the 1860s she made a red-and-white reverse applique quilt with hearts and stars, using both hand and machine applique. It suggests that Narcissa, who lived in south-

Figure 4. Detail of Pineapple quilt made by Narcissa Black of McNairy County, Tennessee, ca. 1870. Collection of State Historical Museum/ Mississippi Department of Archives and History. Photograph by Gib Ford.

western Tennessee, got a sewing machine shortly after the end of the war. (During the same period, she stitched a Log Cabin quilt entirely by hand.) During the next decade, however, she made an intricate Pineapple quilt, entirely appliqued by machine. Perhaps she experimented with the reverse applique in the 1860s, learned to manipulate her machine, and chose to use it for her next appliqued quilt.[39]

By the turn of the century, the sewing machine had ceased to be a status symbol. Most families had them, and women had learned to use them efficiently. With the passing of time, the machine turned into simply that—a machine. When the time came that women took the machine for granted, they—and the magazines they read—once again valued handwork for its own sake. By the end of the nineteenth century, handwork, not machine work, was the status symbol, for the handmade stitch spoke of leisure time and experience with the needle. Given this new attitude, women returned to appliqueing and quilting by hand—quiet, relaxing activities which demonstrated that they had sufficient leisure to sew a fine seam.

Nevertheless, the sewing machine had revolutionized women's attitudes toward their work. Where before they had often complained about the never-ending sewing, they now adopted the machine wholeheartedly. One woman bragged, "I have . . . used it constantly for family sewing; have quilted whole quilts of the largest size and it is still in perfect order, runs like a top, and bids fair to be willed to those who come after me with better powers of production than an unbroken prairie farm."[40]

Few twentieth-century women can imagine the joy with which their great-grandmothers embraced the sewing machine, the first home appliance for women. When contemporary viewers disdain quilts showing machine stitching, they reveal our own age's preference for handwork. A nineteenth-century woman looking at the same quilt would have seen beauty, skill, and comfort, all embodied in the tiny stitches made by the metal workhorse that revolutionized women's sewing.

Notes and References

1. Grace Rogers Cooper, *The Sewing Machine: Its Invention and Development* (Washington, D. C.: Smithsonian Institution Press, 1976), 4.
2. John Kobler, "Mr. Singer's Money Machine," *Saturday Evening Post* (July 14, 1951): 39.
3. Ruth Brandon, *A Capitalist Romance: Singer and the Sewing Machine* (Philadelphia: Lippincott, 1977), 73.
4. Cooper, 219–21.
5. Ibid., 41.
6. Susan Strasser, *Never Done: A History of American Housework* (New York: Pantheon, 1983), 138.

7. Penrose Scull, *From Peddlars to Merchant Princes: A History of Selling in America* (Chicago: Follett, 1967), 187.
8. Broadside, Missouri Historical Society, St. Louis, MO.
9. I. Hale and Co. broadside, Classified file 463, Smithsonian Institution, Washington, D.C.
10. *Godey's Lady's Book* 61 (Sept. 1860): 271.
11. Brandon, 126.
12. *Godey's Lady's Book*, 1863.
13. Brandon, 116.
14. Elaine Hedges, *Hearts and Hands: The Influence of Women and Quilts on American Society* (San Francisco: Quilt Digest Press, 1987), 38.
15. *Godey's Lady's Book* 61 (Sept. 1860): 271.
16. Letter, March 12, 1868, quoted in Harvey Green, *The Light of the Home* (New York: Pantheon, 1983), 80.
17. Nancilu Burdick, letter to author, April 13, 1987.
18. Maria Wicker, St. Louis, to Cyrus Wicker, June 25, 1871. Wicker Collection, Missouri Historical Society, St. Louis.
19. Brandon, 117.
20. Stephen S. Slaughter, *History of a Missouri Farm Family: The O. V. Slaughters, 1700–1944* (Harrison, NY: Harbor Hill, 1978), 55.
21. Brandon, 119.
22. Virginia Gunn, "Quilts for Union Soldiers in the Civil War" in *Uncoverings 1985*, ed. Sally Garoutte (Mill Valley, CA: American Quilt Study Group, 1986), 95.
23. Katherine M. Jones, ed. *Heroines of Dixie* (Westport, CT: Greenwood Press, 1955), 32.
24. Laurel Horton, "South Carolina Quilts and the Civil War" in *Uncoverings 1985*, ed. Sally Garoutte (Mill Valley, CA: American Quilt Study Group, 1986), 60.
25. Jones, 39.
26. Brandon, 122–23.
27. Elaine Hedges, "The 19th-Century Diarist and Her Quilts" in *American Quilts: A Handmade Legacy*, ed. L. Thomas Frye (Oakland, CA: Oakland Museum, 1981), 60.
28. Viriginia Gunn, conversation with author, March 28, 1987.
29. Jonathan Holstein, *The Pieced Quilt: An American Design Tradition* (New York: Galahad Books, 1973), 84.
30. Pieced quilt, Feathered Star, unknown maker, fourth quarter nineteenth century, collection of Robert Cargo, Tuscaloosa, Alabama.
31. Carol Crabbe, letter to author, June 21, 1987.
32. Peggy Potts, letter to author, August 13, 1989.

33. White stitched quilt, made by M. J. Foster, undated, collection of Shelburne Museum, Shelburne, VT.
34. In December, 1905, Rose Oliphant from Lexington, Mississippi, asked *Comfort* for directions for machine quilting. Directions appeared in *Comfort* 18, no. 4 (February 1906). Letter from Katy Christopherson to author, June, 1988.
35. Sybil Lanigan, "Revival of the Patchwork Quilt," *The Ladies' Home Journal* (October 1984): 19, cited in Jeannette Lasansky, *In the Heart of Pennsylvania: 19th and 20th Century Quiltmaking Traditions* (Lewisburg, PA: Oral Traditions Project, 1986), 55.
36. Cuesta Benberry, letter to author, June 8, 1987.
37. Appliqued quilt, Cockscombs and Currant, made by Jane Richey Morelock, collection of Mary K. Morelock Ledford, granddaughter of maker, pictured in Bets Ramsey and Merikay Waldvogel, *Quilts of Tennessee* (Nashville, TN: Rutledge Hill Press, 1986), 46-47.
38. Katy Christopherson and Nancy Hornback, "Logan County Treasure—Found in Kansas" *Back Home in Kentucky* 10, no. 4 (July/August 1987): 48-49.
39. Reverse applique quilt, Pineapple; and pieced quilt, Log Cabin, both in collection of Mississippi State Historical Museum, pictured in Mary Edna Lohrenz and Anita Miller Stamper, *Mississippi Homespun: Nineteenth-Century Textiles and the Women Who Made Them* (Jackson: Mississippi Department of Archives and History, 1989), 5-7.
40. Mills, Betty J., *Calico Chronicle: Texas Women and Their Fashions* (Lubbock: Texas Tech Press, 1985), 84.

Nebraska Quiltmakers: 1870-1940

Elizabeth Weyhrauch Shea and Patricia Cox Crews

The pioneer women and men who settled the grassland plains now called Nebraska faced a harsh environment and long days of hard labor to make the new land their home. Most settlement of the territory occurred after the Civil War and after Nebraska gained its statehood in 1867. Prior to that time millions of people crossed Nebraska en route to Oregon and California, but few regarded Nebraska as a desirable destination. In fact, they often referred to Nebraska as the "Great American Desert."[1]

The growth in the population of the state during the 1860s was spurred by the passage of the Homestead Act in 1862. The construction of the railroads contributed even more to the growth of population in the state during the 1870s. Railroad entrepreneurs launched an intensive advertising campaign promoting Nebraska so they could dispose of the large tracts of lands given to them by the government to finance the construction of the railroads. They produced pamphlets touting Nebraska as almost a "promised land" and sent them to prospective groups in the east and overseas. The pamphlets, traveling exhibits, and promotional lectures convinced thousands of people to head for Nebraska. The population of the state quadrupled during the 1870s. By 1890 the state boasted more than one million inhabitants, many of whom were foreign born.

Many stereotypical images of the frontier environment suggest that it was a man's domain and one where only the most determined and rugged of men could survive. In fact, most of the settlers arriving between 1860 and 1900 were married couples who settled down

---

Elizabeth Weyrauch Shea and Patricia Cox Crews, Department of Textiles, Clothing and Design, College of Home Economics, University of Nebraska, Lincoln NE 68583-0802

to farm and raise families. Life in the new land was harsh and challenging, physically and emotionally. Sex roles, particularly for women, often were blurred by necessity as frontier women took on whatever work was necessary in the field, as well as their traditional domain, the home.

Recent scholarship describes the importance of women's contributions in forming frontier society.[2] Yet, much research remains to be done to fully document women's role in the settlement of the West.

Data Collection and Analysis

The Lincoln Quilters Guild initiated the Nebraska Quilt Project in 1985. The paucity of information about midwestern quiltmaking traditions led to a desire to document existing quilts, particularly surviving nineteenth- and early twentieth-century quilts before the quilts were worn out or sold to buyers outside the state. To prepare for the project, twenty members of the Lincoln Quilters Guild attended training sessions on photography, the context of folk art in Nebraska, oral interview techniques, fiber and fabric analysis, and the documentation and dating of quilts. In this way, a core group of Guild members became trained "para-professionals" who collected data during the Nebraska Quilt History Days under the supervision of Frances Best, the project director. The twenty sites selected for the Quilt History Days represented the ethnic, geographic, and economic diversity of the state. Eighty-two of the ninety-three counties in Nebraska were represented in the survey, providing a broad sampling of the state's quiltmakers and quilts for this study. The trained volunteers registered over 1,000 quiltmakers and nearly 4,000 quilts between April 27, 1987 and June 15, 1988.

The Quilt History Days were conducted according to procedures modeled after those successfully used in other states and are described in detail elsewhere.[3] Information about the quiltmaker's life, motivations, and quiltmaking practices garnered from the questionnaires provided the major source of data for this study. In addition, project members conducted ninety-four taped interviews with quiltmakers who were willing to share their practices and life experiences or quilt owners who could shed light on the lives and practices of early quiltmakers. The transcribed oral interviews served as a source of anecdotal information about Nebraska quiltmakers.

On the basis of the analysis and interpretation of this large body of data, a demographic profile of Nebraska quiltmakers emerged as well as insights into their quiltmaking practices and motivations for quiltmaking.[4] This paper summarizes those findings and offers our interpretations of them.

A Demographic Profile

The majority of Nebraska quiltmakers were rural women with grade school educations living on farms or in small communities. Most married which was not surprising as most women of the era eventually married.[5] As one Nebraska quiltmaker relates,

> Well, it was just part of being. . . . The women in those days . . . when they grew up married. . . . If you weren't married your father or brother had to support you and take care of you. It was very rare that a woman remained unmarried. And so, to prepare yourself for marriage and having a home and children, you learned to sew and to cook, and it was just part of your life.[6]

Most Nebraska quiltmakers had two to four children, the norm for American women between 1870 and 1950.[7] Although some novelists and historians characterized the plains pioneer woman as mother of ten to twelve children, most women settling the Plains during the last quarter of the nineteenth century had only three to four children.[8] The typical Nebraska quiltmaker was no exception; her frontier household usually consisted of herself, her husband, and a few children living together. While some Nebraska quiltmakers did have large families, as many as fourteen to sixteen children, most did not.

Nebraska quiltmakers participated in a variety of occupations including teaching, dressmaking, farming, ranching, nursing, retailing (hardware stores, general stores, antiques stores, and department stores), domestic services (housekeeper, hired girl), and clerical services. A few were telephone operators, beauticians, or bookbinders. One was a postmistress. The majority were ranch wives, farmwives, or housewives, as were most women of the nineteenth and first half of the twentieth century. Of the Nebraska quiltmakers who worked outside the home, most were teachers or dressmakers. This reflects the times: In 1880, four-fifths of all American women engaged in non-farm employment worked as teachers, servants and laundresses, clerks and salespeople, dressmakers, milliners, and seamstresses.[9] The majority of white working women throughout the nineteenth and first half of the twentieth century were young and single; women usually abandoned or were required to quit work for pay when they married.[10] A number of Nebraska quiltmakers mentioned that they, too, gave up paid work when they married.

The largest identified ethnic group within Nebraska quiltmakers were Germans followed by English, Czech, Irish, Scotch, Danish, Swedish, and Norwegian. The ethnic background of the quiltmakers reflects the ethnic background of Nebraska's immigrants in the late 1800s, most of whom were Germans followed by smaller but significant percentages of Swedes, Irish, Czechs, and Danes.[11] Many of the quiltmakers or their parents came to Nebraska following the American Civil War when a wave of migration populated the remaining western territories. This movement started during the 1870s and subsided by the 1890s when almost all of the railroad lands and public lands had been transferred to private ownership. One quiltmaker's family came to Nebraska following the Civil War with a colony settling in Gibbon in 1871. A grandson, Leroy Walker, describes their experience as follows:

> Colonel Thorp got a bunch of people together by advertising. They all got on the train in the eastern states, all strangers to each other, and they came west and settled at Gibbon. All nationalities: Irish, English, just whoever happened to answer the ads. . . . Grandfather [a Civil War veteran] when he came to Gibbon had twenty dollars in his pocket, not enough to get out of there so he had to stay [in Nebraska]. Besides Grandma told him this was our last move, because every time they'd moved they got poorer and poorer and poorer.[12]

Religious groups were active in the settlement of Nebraska during those years. For example, Lutheran pastors led many groups of Scandinavian immigrants; Congregationalists founded York; and the Mennonite leader, Peter Jansen, helped establish several Mennonnite communities near Lincoln.[13] Most Nebraska quiltmakers were

Methodists or Lutherans. Of the remaining quiltmakers, most identified themselves as Catholic, Presbyterian, Christian, Congregational, Baptist, or Mennonite. Methodist and Lutheran religious perferences are generally associated with those of English, German, and Scandinavian descent, while Catholicism is often associated with those of Czech and Irish descent.

Although Nebraska had a diverse population in which national or religious groups frequently dominated rural communities and maintained their language and customs, neither the project members nor the researchers observed strong ethnic influences on quilt construction and patterns in the quilts and quiltmaking practices of Nebraska quiltmakers. If distinctive quiltmaking traditions existed among the immigrants when they arrived, they did not survive for long. In fact, differences may not have existed at all. According to family tradition, Mary Novotny Lahowetz pieced a Basket quilt in Bohemia in the 1850s then quilted it after her arrival in America. It is similar in pattern and construction to other Nebraska-made pieced quilts of the period. Her quilt and another one made by a German quiltmaker for her brother traveling to America stand as evidence that immigrant women not only brought the necessary sewing skills for quiltmaking with them to America, they brought pieced blocks and even quilts to their new homes. If any differences in quilt styles and construction techniques existed, the sharing of patterns and construction techniques quickly obscured them.

Motivations for Quiltmaking

The majority of Nebraska quiltmakers started quiltmaking as a form of self-expression and a pastime that they enjoyed. Quiltmaking allowed women to escape the rigors and drabness of their everyday routines into a kaleidoscopic world of color. The personal satisfaction derived from this pastime was an important motivation for Amelia Barbe who continued piecing quilts even after she started to lose her eyesight. Her granddaughter relates:

> I have some of her tops that she pieced together on the treadle sewing machine after she lost most of her eyesight. She was blind in one eye and had about only twenty per cent vision in the other eye, but she

kept on piecing. Some of the pieces don't meet, some of the seams kind of go off all over the place, but it's interesting that she kept on trying to do the handiwork after she lost her eyesight.[14]

Ellen Maxwell found quiltmaking therapeutic. She made a crazy quilt to overcome grief following the death of her baby girl from diphtheria during an epidemic in the winter of 1892. According to her granddaughter:

> Grandmother was so laid out by the death that she was unable to go on with her life. And so Grandpa ran or took a horse over to the neighboring couple, an older couple, who had lost their only child many years ago. [The neighbor] gathered up scraps of velvet and silk and old linsey-wool and strands of thread and showed Grandma how to fashion pieces and then embroider flowers and birds and so forth on it. [Grandma] patiently put them together.... She tacked the flowers or fruit from a seed catalog and then embroidered over it, then picked out the paper behind. That's how they did, they didn't have patterns in those days you know. And so, she feather-stitched around each piece.... Each night she would work by the light of the lamp.... Gradually she got better.... Grandma got hold of her life again and finished the quilt and folded it up and put it away.... When we'd ask to see the quilt, she'd get it out, but she never used it because the memory in each scrap would just tell her about her baby daughter.[15]

Some quiltmakers quilted because they needed warm bedding, and they found quiltmaking an economical way to meet this need. Some quilted to demonstrate their thriftiness and careful use of scarce resources. Perhaps the words of Genevieve Young from Nebraska City best express many quiltmaker's reasons for saving scraps.

> I have collected fabrics all my life, and I just never thought it was wise to throw away even an inch of fabric. I always collected all of the tiny pieces that nobody else wanted, and I always thought it would be awfully nice if you could just put all those pieces, roll them all together like you do pie dough, then roll them out and have one piece.[16]

Others made quilts because they had little money to do other things. According to her family, Gertrude Scudder made her Trip Around the World quilt during the Depression of the 1930s "because you didn't have any money ... she made quilts."[17]

Although many maintain the popular notion that pieced quilts were born out of hardship and economic necessity, most Nebraska quiltmakers did not cite that motivation. Some quilts are so complex and the needlework so fine that it is clear that the quiltmakers did not cite that motivation. Some quilts are so complex and the needlework so fine that it is clear that the quiltmakers did not hastily assemble them to provide warm bedding. Instead, the quiltmakers created objects of beauty and pride that displayed their exquisite needlework skills and artistic abilities. Certainly pioneer values of thriftiness and industriousness encouraged virtuous women to devote their free time to quiltmaking or other forms of needlework, but necessity was not the quiltmaker's major reason for making quilts. Instead, most respondents noted that the reason for making quilts was the pleasure and satisfaction derived from making useful and beautiful items for their families.

For rural American women, especially those settling the frontier, there were few opportunities for artistic expression. Painting, sculpture, and other fine arts were considered far too frivolous for most rural women to undertake. Quiltmaking, which produced a useful item for their families, afforded women an acceptable avenue of creative expression. From the numbers of outstanding quilts that have survived, it is clear that many women exercised this option.

Special occasions such as birthdays, graduations, marriages, and births prompted a great deal of quiltmaking. Of these, weddings and births, occasions that mark new beginnings, inspired the most quiltmaking. Family members usually received the quilts made for these occasions. Lena Burger of De Witt described the number of quilts that she made for members of her family when they married. "All twenty of my grandchildren, they all got their quilt, or are getting it. When they get married they get their quilt."[18]

Quiltmaking Practices

In general, quiltmaking was a lifelong activity. The hardships of relocation and settlement in a sometimes hostile land did not interrupt quiltmaking activities for long, if at all. For example, Clarissa Griswold made a beautiful crazy quilt while she sat her homestead claim in Sioux County, Nebraska, between 1885 and 1886. Sophia Hinrichs and her daughter, Helena Hinrichs Prange, provide yet another example of the many women who made quilts while living under most unfavorable conditions during homesteading years. They pieced their fan quilt while living in a dark, dank dugout, the temporary home of many plains pioneer families.

Some women started to make quilts as children because, in rural households, children and adolescents were expected to participate in the household work of their families. Household responsibilities included learning needlework skills. Throughout the nineteenth century, girls frequently learned to sew before they learned to read, and they sometimes pieced simple quilt blocks at an early age, as young as two or three, to practice and improve their sewing skills.[19] Many quiltmakers related stories about their childhood quiltmaking experiences. Belle Frasier of Parks, Nebraska, the youngest quiltmaker included in this survey, started her first quilt when she was three and a half years old. It was a simple Four Patch. "Just little squares," as she described it. "My mother would cut them out and pin them together and mark where I was supposed to sew."[20] Peg Kildare of Ogallala remembers how her mother insisted every afternoon that I sit down at a certain time and put that quilt together. "Oh, I got so I hated it . . . but she made me finish. . . . I had to sit there, and now I'm glad she did because I never start anything but what I finish it."[21] Another quiltmaker said, "I think my mother learned me to quilt when I was twelve years old. She started me out sewing carpet rags. Just kept on, kept on until I learned to quilt."[22]

These anecdotes illustrate that quiltmaking skills, like most needlework skills, were transmitted by adult women to young girls. Almost seventy per cent of the quiltmakers surveyed learned their quiltmaking skills from family members, usually mothers, but occasionally from grandmothers, aunts, or sisters. While about twenty per cent indicated that they taught themselves to quilt, they probably learned the necessary sewing skills from other women. Only two women indicated that they learned to make quilts in classes. Quiltmaking in Nebraska reflects a widespread feminine skill usually transmitted from mother to daughter in the home. While this may be typical of the transferral of quiltmaking skills in rural families across America during the time, it contrasts with the eastern tradition in affluent urban families where girls often learned needlework skills through special ornamental needlework classes in private finishing schools or boarding schools.[23]

While some quiltmakers started to quilt as children under their mother's close supervision, the majority of Nebraska quiltmakers made their first quilts as young adults. Many young adults made their first quilts for their dowries or to accommodate the needs of their young families.

Although the majority of Nebraska quiltmakers started to quilt as young adults, there were a few who began later in life (after sixty years of age). One of these, Marie Jahnke of Bancroft, noted,

> I lived on the farm for thirty-five years. . . . It was a little while before I moved to town when I started quilting. When my husband quit farming then I didn't have to help as much, but otherwise I was always out there helping him with everything, plus going to work everyday.[24]

Surprisingly, about one-third of the Nebraska women surveyed made most of their quilts during mid-life when they had children at home. Although they had many demands on their time during these years, they found time to quilt. Some quiltmakers pieced their quilts during spare moments while doing other farm work, such as Ardyth Triplette, an Ogallala quiltmaker, who said,

> I spend my whole life waiting on men because I drive a corn truck and bean truck, and it seems like you spend all day settin' in line to dump. And so I just take my quilt box with me and I work 'em sittin' in the truck.[25]

Almost an equal number indicated that they made most of their quilts after their children were grown. They had more time to devote to quiltmaking during those years. In addition, many women expressed a desire to create something for which they would be remembered, an heirloom to be passed down to family members.

Some women quilted into their eighties, and a few women were ninety years old when they completed their quilts. Whether the motivation to quilt was to satisfy their desire to create a thing of beauty for themselves or their descendants, to satisfy their sense of the proper way to use their time and scarce resources, or to provide warm bedding for their families, many women made quilts throughout their lives.

Many Nebraska quiltmakers believed they made their best quilts after their children were grown. They could devote more time to quiltmaking, and they had a lifetime of experience in quiltmaking and sewing to apply to the task. Surprisingly, an equal number of quiltmakers believed they made their best quilts during mid-life when their children were at home. Although women had fewer responsibilities and demands on their time when younger and preparing quilts for their dowries, few women thought they made their best quilts as young adults. Sewing was a measure of a woman's ability as a homemaker and the consummate feminine skill during the nineteenth century. Apparently most women believed that their skills improved over the years and, of equal importance, they continued to devote the time required for meticulously crafted quilts although burdened by a multitude of chores as farmwives and mothers.

When asked about the frequency of quiltmaking, seventy per cent responded that they quilted frequently, while thirty per cent quilted on an infrequent basis. The frequency of quiltmaking often depended upon factors like the time of year, how much time was available to quilt, and the occasion for which the quilt was made. An upcoming birth, marriage, or high-school graduation in the family often provided the impetus for more frequent quiltmaking. The time of year affected the frequency of quiltmaking for those who lived on farms because seasonal work influenced the amount of time available for needlework. Seasonal responsibilities, especially during the spring, summer, and fall, proved particularly demanding. Wintertime was frequently mentioned by quiltmakers as the time of year that they could devote to their quiltmaking activities. But women made quilts year round and in many unlikely settings. Irene Alexander recalls that her mother always wanted her children to have something to do while they were out herding the cows. "We would piece the blocks by hand and use our time that way. We also did embroidery work while we were there."[26]

Very few Nebraska quiltmakers made over one hundred quilts; most made fewer than fifty quilts and many made fewer than ten quilts. However, some women were truly prolific. Minnie Geise Sukraw made about 1,300 tied quilts, largely for overseas relief.[27] While tied quilts took less time than those that were quilted, this accomplishment is nonetheless remarkable.

Quiltmaking is a time-consuming task. Although some quilts were completed in six months and others spanned a life time, the average

Nebraska quiltmaker completed a quilt in about two years. In general, quiltmakers devoted the time necessary to make products that reflected meticulous care and craftsmanship, and that would reflect well on their needlework skills. The amount of time required to produce each quilt is an argument against the popular notion that the major impetus for quilting during the nineteenth century was the urgent need for warm bedding by penniless settlers who had little other than scraps and rags from which to make their quilts.

Nebraska quiltmakers purchased and used about as much new fabric as dressmaker cuttings or scraps. This was apparent in the number of registered quilts that had a matching sashing, border, or backing; the quantities of material required for this effect were more likely purchased than available from cuttings or scraps. The colorful and varied prints in the pieced blocks were usually the only parts of the quilts that came from dressmaking cuttings. Because pieced quilts effectively used these scraps, Nebraska quiltmakers made pieced quilts in far greater numbers than applique quilts which generally required larger amounts of matching fabrics. The bountiful number of pieced quilts was noted in the North Carolina survey for similar reasons.[28] Worn-out clothing was rarely used by Nebraska quiltmakers. However, recycled flour, salt, sugar, tobacco, and feed sacks sometimes appear in quilts, and, on occasion, old neckties and political ribbons.

Most Nebraska quiltmakers named no favorite pattern according to responses on the survey forms. However, those few who identified a favorite pattern usually mentioned the Double Wedding Ring, Dresden Plate, or Grandmother's Flower Garden. More Double Wedding Ring and Gradmother's Flower Garden quilts were registered in the state during the Nebraska Quilt Project than any other patterns, which further supports their favored status among Nebraska quiltmakers.[29] When asked why a pattern was a particular favorite, responses included that it was economical to make (Double Wedding Ring, Friendship, and Log Cabin), colorful (Nine Patch), appropriate for grandchildren (Sunbonnet Sue and Overall Boys), and beautiful and meaningful to them (Double Wedding Ring). When Abba Jane Johnston found a pattern that suited her, the Barn Raising variation of the Log Cabin, she "never strayed from it." According to her great-granddaughter:

It was a trait that carried through into many aspects of her life and gave real meaning to the word *method* in Methodist. She was not known for deviating from the straight and narrow! But she was known for her good deeds, and no doubt her sewing skills came in especially handy when she stitched up the lip of a woman cut in a butchering accident—a legendary story in the family.[30]

Family, friends, and neighbors were among the most often mentioned sources of patterns for Nebraska quilts. Quiltmakers exchanged patterns much as they traded recipes. During the 1930s and 1940s Louise Howey of Lincoln, exchanged patterns with about twenty-five quiltmakers across the United States and Canada through round robins.[31] Another important source of patterns among quiltmakers was the print media: books, women's magazines, and newspapers. Surprisingly, almost a quarter of the respondents indicated that the quilts were original designs. However, careful scrutiny of the quilts identified as a quiltmaker's own design showed that over half of them were signature, friendship, or crazy quilts, and a third were variations of traditional designs. Only a few would be regarded as truly original designs.

Nearly two-thirds of the quilts registered were quilted by the quiltmaker herself rather than by someone else. This is not surprising since quiltmakers, like many artists, nurture the vision of their quilts from selection of the pattern to completion in the quilting frame. Therefore, they wanted to control each step of their quilt's development from the first to the last stitch. Some women preferred to quilt alone because they were very particular and did not want irregular quilting stitches to spoil their carefully pieced or appliqued tops. When asked if she ever quilted with groups, Jessie Hervert of Kearney replied, "No, I like to make the stitches myself. Even the twins never helped me stitch my quilts. Because not that they couldn't do it good enough, but because I don't sew like they sew."[32] When asked if she quilted for other people, Peg Kildare responded, "Just for the senior citizens. But my own quilts, I do all my own quilting."[33]

Distance between neighbors, farm duties, and parenting responsibilities sometimes required quiltmakers to quilt alone. Mary Catherine Ray Newkirk, for example, lived in Washington County, west of Blair. In 1877, she came from Effingham, Illinois, with her seven brothers and sisters. They didn't have a social life at all because they were miles from their nearest neighbors and because "they struggled to live and keep warm and not [let] anyone get sick."[34]

While Nebraska quiltmakers spent many hours quilting alone, some also participated in quiltmaking activities for fellowship and fundraising at church, community clubs, and even in their homes. The majority of those who quilted with groups usually did so in church groups or a friend's home perhaps because of similar traditions, language, interests, and philosophies. Katheryn Thomsen of Omaha remembers when she lived in the country how her mother would have quilting parties. "It was complete enjoyment for these people to come over. . . . Sometimes after they quit my mom would go over and look at the quilting and she would take out [stitches made by] the person in the club who made large stitches."[35] Obviously fellowship was more important than progress in the quilting. Her mother held the parties despite the fact that some of the quilting that occurred did not meet her standards. Lois Hanson remembers, as a girl growing up in Holdrege, that the women in her mother's clubs did a lot of quilting together. "They were [quilting] mostly for pleasure, and I suppose they needed the quilts. It was a friendship thing where you got your neighbors together and visited and quilted."[36]

Summary

Quiltmaking in Nebraska was a practice of thriftiness, a well-regarded feminine pastime, and an enduring form of self-expression. Nebraskans prided themselves in their hard work, frugality, and resourcefulness. Their quiltmaking clearly reflected these values. Consequently, quiltmaking remained a popular activity among rural women throughout the years of Nebraska's settlement and development and well into the twentieth century. Despite the difficulties and hardships which Nebraska women surely encountered during the early years of settlement, they found time for quiltmaking.

The quilts that Nebraska quiltmakers made and their reasons for making them mirror women's many and varied roles. As nurturers, women made quilts for their own infants and grandchildren; as social communicators, women made friendship, signature, and album quilts for their friends and families; as moral guardians of the family, women made quilts to raise funds for their churches and for other worthwhile causes; as accomplished seamstresses, women made quilts with incredible numbers of pieces and quilted them with stitches so tiny that they sometimes require a magnifying glass to see. Their quilts are valuable artifacts because they elicit memories of their makers, family members, and special occasions; because they are symbols of family heritage and traditions; and because they are beautiful examples of women's folk art.

Acknowledgments

We extend thanks to the National Endowment for the Arts, The American/International Quilt Association, The Center for Great Plains Studies, and The University of Nebraska-Lincoln for their financial support of this research. And, to the dedicated volunteers of the Nebraska Quilt Project whose tireless efforts made this research possible, we congratulate you on a job well done.

Notes and References

1. James C. Olson, *History of Nebraska* (Lincoln: University of Nebraska Press, 1966).
2. Glenda Riley, "Women on the Great Plains: Recent Developments in Research," *Great Plains Quarterly* 5 (Spring 1985): 81-92.
3. Joseph F. Stonuey and Patricia Cox Crews, "The Nebraska Quilt History Project: Interpretations of Selected Parameters" in *Uncoverings* 1988, ed. Laurel Horton (San Francisco: American Quilt Study Group, 1989), 154-55.
4. Elizabeth Weyhrauch Shea, "The Nebraska Quiltmaker" Masters thesis (University of Nebraska-Lincoln, 1989), 67-109.
5. Andrew J. Cherlin, *Marriage, Divorce, Remarriage* (Cambridge: Harvard University Press, 1981), 20-21.
6. Clara Wertz, taped interview, Lincoln NE, June 11, 1988.
7. Cherlin, 20-21.
8. Julie Roy Jeffrey, *Frontier Women: The Trans-Mississippi West, 1840-1880* (New York: Hill and Wang, 1979), 57-58.
9. Carl N. Degler, *At Odds: Women and the Family in America from the Revolution to the Present* (Oxford: Oxford University Press, 1980), 377.

10. Ibid., 383.
11. Olson, 173.
12. Leroy Walker, taped interview, Kearney NE, June 24, 1987.
13. Olson, 173.
14. Sandra Anderson, taped interview, Lincoln NE, May 25, 1988.
15. Dorothy Boettner, taped interview, Wahoo NE, August 28, 1987.
16. Genevieve Young, taped interview, Nebraska City NE, September 11, 1987.
17. Ruth Sisler, taped interview, Kearney NE, June 24, 1987.
18. Lena Burger, taped interview, Dorchester NE, May 30, 1987.
19. Pat Ferrero, Elaine Hedges, and Julie Silber, *Hearts and Hands: The Influence of Women and Quilts on American Society* (San Francisco: Quilt Digest Press, 1987), 16–21.
20. Edith Belle Sims Frasier, taped interview, Benkelman NE, April 29, 1987.
21. Peg Kildare, taped interview, Ogallala NE, April 27, 1987.
22. Ruth Davidson, taped interview, Nebraska City NE, September 11, 1987.
23. Susan Burrows Swan, "Molding the Accomplished Miss," in *Plain and Fancy*, (New York: Holt, Rinehart and Winston, 1977), 44–83.
24. Marie Jahnke, taped interview, Bancroft NE, July 20, 1987.
25. Ardyth Triplette, taped interview, Ogallala NE, April 27, 1987.
26. Irene Alexander, taped interview, Lincoln NE, July 13, 1988.
27. Miriam Sukraw, survey forms for quilt no. 2364 made by Minnie Geise Sukraw.
28. Kathlyn F. Sullivan, "Pieced and Plentiful," *North Carolina Quilts*, ed. Ruth Haislip Roberson (Chapel Hill: University of North Carolina Press, 1988), 99.
29. Stonuey and Crews, 160.
30. Mary Oba, supplemental information for quilt nos. 380–386.
31. Louise Howey, taped interview, Lincoln NE, October 30, 1987.
32. Jessie Hervert, taped interview, Kearney NE, June 24, 1987.
33. Kildare, interview.
34. Mary Anderson, taped interview, Blair NE, July 22, 1987.
35. Katheryn Thomsen, taped interview, Bancroft NE, July 20, 1987.
36. Lois Hanson, taped interview, Lincoln NE, May 25, 1988.

The Ladies Aid of Hope Lutheran Church

Debra Ballard

I was very excited in the fall of 1988 when my grandmother, Louise Mathieson, gave me a large box containing quilt templates, quilt patterns, and the wrappers from old Mountain Mist quilt batts. She told me that most of these items had been used by the Ladies Aid of Hope Lutheran Church over the period of more than fifty years that the group has been meeting to quilt. Because of my own love for quilting and because I know many of these women, the gift sparked my interest in the group. I began to seek out the women in order to better understand why they had quilted together for so many years.

Hope Lutheran Church was formed in 1914 in the small farming community of Rhodes, in Gladwin County, Michigan. The founders, descendants of Hanover Germans who came to America in the 1850s and settled in Ohio, were hard-working people who braved hardships to begin a new way of life in Michigan. Farmland in Ohio had become priced out of reach for many people. Families from the Ohio farmlands moved to Michigan in the early 1900s, where land could be bought cheaply or homesteaded. Homesteading was done on land which had been cleared by loggers and abandoned. On April 23, 1914, nine men with high hopes signed the charter for the new church. They named it Hope Lutheran Church in memory of the church which many had attended since childhood in Hamler, Ohio. The charter members included Dietrich Schaard, Henry Mohrmann, Henry Ehlers, Sr., Henry Ehlers, Jr., Henry Lindhorst, Carl Meyer, William Ehlers, Fred Schaard, and George Westenfeld.[1]

Debra Ballard, 5307 Plainfield Street, Midland MI 48640

Figure 1. Hope Lutheran Church at the time of its purchase in 1914. The fence kept cattle away from the church. (Photo courtesy of Emma Rabe.)

In the early days of the church only the men held offices. The women played a minimal role in the church. The prevailing attitude of the day was that a woman's place was at home raising the children. This was no easy task. While caring for the children, keeping house, and planting and tending a large garden, a woman also helped her husband in the barn and fields. Families did not have the extra money to hire help and often traded work with one another.

In 1938 the Reverend Alfred Schum and his wife, Irma, came to the church in Rhodes. Mr. and Mrs. Schum had no children, and both devoted themselves to the church. Irma was very interested in the women of the church and their activities. She organized a quilting group to provide an opportunity for the women to socialize. According to Louise Mathieson, "she [Irma Schum] thought that would be a nice thing to do for the women to get together 'cause the women didn't get out very often. You didn't go to the movies or dances or anything. And you didn't have a televison. They had radios and that was it. They were stuck right on the farms. Most of them were busy having a family, raising a family."[2]

Mrs. Schum was not a quilter herself but thoroughly enjoyed organizing the group and meeting with the women.

By the late 1930s the village of Rhodes had grown into a thriving small town. It consisted of a livery and blacksmith shop, a pool room, a bank, a lunch room and ice cream parlor, a garage and grain elevator, a post office, a hardware store, a general store, a hotel, a factory which manufactured bean-picking machines, and a pickle station. (The farmers brought their pickles to the station to be weighed and sorted before being sold to the canning factories.) Hope Lutheran Church was an important part of the community life of Rhodes, and the quiltings of the Ladies Aid were the primary social event of each week.

Often many days would pass before a woman might even have a chance to talk to another woman. Until the late 1950s many farms in Gladwin County did not have telephones. Women usually had to walk some distance to see their neighbors. The Ladies Aid gave the women a reason to come together to enjoy themselves and each other.

Quilting was a relief from the male-dominated world. The women came together as equals. They could make all decisions regarding their quilting and how to spend the money they earned. It must have been very satisfying for these women to work as a group for the good of their church without having to consult with the men. With all the work the women had to do each day there was little time for relaxation. Quilting allowed the women time for themselves.

The women developed deep and intimate friendships while working around the quilting frame. These friendships have lasted lifetimes. Women willingly offered each other comfort and support through the trials of day-to-day living. Talk was easy around the frame whether it centered on how to can peaches, what to do with a colicky baby, or how to deal with a demanding husband. Young women learned from the older, more experienced women. In this small, rural community the Ladies Aid offered women a welcome haven from the rigors of farm life. The women, at times, had to bring their children when they went quilting. Louise Krevinghaus recalled young children playing under the quilts and their heads pushing up on the quilts. The quilters would "thunk" the children's heads with their thimbles in fun.

In 1939 the women of the church, including their friends and neighbors in Rhodes, presented Mr. and Mrs. Schum with a quilt. They chose the Colonial Girl, a favorite pattern of the 1930s, for the quilt. Sarah Witte, Clara Rabe, and Mary Keller appliqued each block with a buttonhole stitch in variegated threads. The names of thirty women were embroidered on the quilt. The ten blocks on the inside of the quilt each contain two embroidered names while only one name appears on each of the outside blocks. Several family names are repeated on the quilt reflecting work done by two generations of the Witte, Rabe, Ehlers, Brumley, and LaFrenier families. The names of Lena LaFrenier, my paternal great-grandmother, and her two daughters, Louise Mathieson and Dorothy LaFrenier, all appear on the quilt. It was common for a mother, along with her daughters and daughters-in-law, to belong to Hope Lutheran Church, and thus, to the Ladies Aid and the quilting group. After the quilt was put together the group met to do the quilting. The quilt shows wear from the years of use by the Schums. Mrs. Lillian Meyer, a lifelong member of the church, accepted the quilt after the Schums died.[3]

On January 26, 1940, the women of the church formally became the Ladies Aid Society of Hope Lutheran Congregation of Rhodes, Michigan. Irma Schum served as the first president of the group. Seventeen women attended the first formal meeting held at the church. The constitution states the objective of the group: "That we may become more active and systematic in the fulfillment of our duties as Christians and members of the above mentioned congregation." Members fulfilled their duties using the money made through quilting and sewing for their church. The women also donated help to their neighbors whenever it was needed. The women met formally the first Wednesday of each month at a member's home for a business meeting and a lunch furnished by the hostess. The Ladies Aid continues to meet in this same manner today.

Besides the formal monthly meetings the women met one day a week in members' homes to quilt. Each woman brought a dish to pass for lunch. It was often the only day off the farm for many of the women, and they describe it as a day of pure fun. A favorite place to quilt was the home of Mrs. Ida Witte, or "Grandma Witte" as her friends still remember her. Her home had a large front room

Figure 2. The women of the Ladies Aid, ca. 1950, at the home of Mrs. Ida Witte. Seated from left to right: Louise Mathieson, Margaret Labo, Minnie Witte, Edna Peters, Leola Krevinghaus, Elma Krueger, Louise Palmer, Clara Rabe, Nettie Palmer, Eleanor Labo, Ida Witte, Anna Ehlers. (Photo courtesy of Louise Mathieson.)

that could easily accommodate the quilt frame. All of her children were married and living on their own, so there was no one to disturb the quilt between quilting days. Clara Rabe and Anna Ehlers were two of her daughters; Sara Witte and Minnie Witte were her daughters-in-law. All quilted with the group through the 1960s and 1970s.

All of the women interviewed mentioned the good times they had at the quiltings. Theresa Lindhurst went to the quiltings for "the camaraderie and to get to know my neighbors better. They'd laugh so much at times they couldn't even sew." She shared a lemon pie story that still brings a smile to her face. On April Fool's Day someone brought a beautiful lemon pie for lunch and everyone had a little piece of it. Instead of adding sugar the maker deliberately substituted salt as a joke. Everyone stayed puckered up that day.[4]

Mrs. Elma Krueger and her daughter Louise felt a strong commitment to the group. While Louise was still attending high school, the school bus would drop her off at Grandma Witte's house on quilting days so she could quilt with her mother and the Ladies Aid. Once Minnie Witte rode with the mailman to get there. Several women said they had walked knee-deep in mud and snow to get to the quiltings.

Paul and Minnie Witte were active members of the church, and Minnie fondly remembers the quiltings. She did not begin to quilt until after she was married. She routinely used flour and sugar sacks for the backs of her quilts and for the pieced tops. She made slips for herself and her daughters from bleached flour sacks, trimming them with bits of lace.[5]

The new Ladies Aid group kept formal minutes beginning in January 1940. These records regularly mention quilting. Although the women did not raffle the quilts they made, as it was against the policy of the church, they were able to sell their quilts and their quilting skills. The ladies quilted for both members and non-members. They charged members $.50 for a 150-yard spool of thread, and non-members $1.00 for a 150-yard spool. In March 1940 they charged $5.00 to piece a quilt plus $1.00 for the quilting. In February 1941 a motion was made to sell two quilts the women had made for a combined cost of $15.00. In March they were offered and accepted $14.00 for the two quilts instead of their original asking price.[6]

Along with quilting, the women of the Ladies Aid also stripped feathers for feather beds. This involved taking the hard spine out of each feather. Many of the older members continued to use feather beds until recently. Old feather ticks can still be found in many attics today. In 1941, the Ladies Aid charged 50 cents for stripping feathers one full day for a member of the group. Cash was in short supply, and bartering was used in many transactions. Firewood, eggs, milk, and labor were freely traded and given to those who were in need. In talking with the women, though, all said they never felt poor at that time because "everyone else was in the same fix."

The Ladies Aid used the money they earned solely for the church and church-related projects. The ledger shows total earning of $99.70 for 1941. Of this amount $81.43 was earned from quilting. A history written to commemorate the seventy-fifth anniversary of the church states "the women of the church have contributed greatly, both financially and spiritually, toward our church and have unfailingly taken on projects and restoration work when it was asked of them."

Through the years the women repeatedly purchased paint for the church and the rectory. They also paid for a new roof, basement flooring, windows, carpeting, and curtains. They bought hams and turkeys for the annual mother-daughter banquet and for church picnics. They paid for flowers for the alter and bulbs for the church grounds. They purchased choir robes and paid to have them dry-cleaned. During World War II they prepared "soldiers boxes" for those in service, sending the men mittens, socks, and canned food.[7]

The quilts made by the Ladies Aid were of a variety of patterns, but favorites included the Double Wedding Ring and the Lone Star. The women frequently traded patterns and occasionally purchased new ones. Patterns could be ordered through the *Bay City Times*, the local newspaper. The women copied patterns from quilts they saw and admired. Emma Rabe saw a Single Irish Chain quilt hanging on a neighbor's clothesline when she was fourteen years old. She remembered that quilt, and years later she made herself a copy. When Theresa Lindhurst saw a pattern she liked she would draw it out on paper as soon as she got home. She is very competent at drafting patterns and has never purchased a quilt pattern. Women also called on their husbands to help draft patterns. Mary Keller's husband Wes drafted all her quilt patterns through her many years of quilting.

Men supported women's quilting activities in other ways. Emma Rabe, now 93 years old, and her husband, Otto, were married on January 6, 1916. On January 26 of that year they moved from Ohio to Gladwin County. They both worked to clear brush and pull stumps to prepare the land for planting. When Emma was a young wife and mother her stepmother asked Emma why her quilt frame was not set up. Emma explained that she didn't have time for fancy quilting; she had to help Otto keep the cows out of the corn. In later years, when Emma had time to quilt, she put together a make-shift frame, balancing it on kitchen chairs. When her father saw her quilting on the home-made frame, he went outside, picked up leftover lumber from a grainery he and Otto were building, and made Emma a better quilt frame. She still uses that frame today.[8]

The women donated most of the materials for their quilts. They used feed sacks, scraps left from sewing clothes, and worn clothes that could be cut apart. When the women purchased materials for quilting or embroidery work, they often made their purchases at the general store owned by my grandparents, John and Louise Mathieson. The Ladies Aid ledger for December 1940 shows an expenditure of $1.47 for material, batting, and thread. In 1942 the group spent $1.39 for five yards of a rose-and-blue print.[9]

Quilt blocks and complete quilt tops were sometimes donated to the group to be quilted and sold. On one occasion, a member asked if the Ladies Aid would like to buy an applique top that she had decided not to complete. The Ladies Aid members discussed whether or not to buy the quilt kit. One mentioned that all the pieces to be appliqued were already cut out. One of the younger members spoke up and suggested that it was not an advantage to have the pieces cut out. The number on the side of each piece that matched the number on the quilt top had been cut off, making the matching of the pieces nearly impossible. The majority voted to purchase the top. Then the fun began. Because all the numbers on the applique pieces had been cut off, there was no method for matching the applique pieces to the appropriate places on the quilt top. It was like a giant jigsaw puzzle. The Ladies Aid spent long hours to solve the puzzle of the applique quilt top. Eventually the top was completed, quilted, and sold.[10]

The Ladies Aid made many quilts for charity. The group made lap robes for residents of rest homes. Following World War II there was a call for quilts to be sent to Europe.[11] The women eagerly heeded the call and made durable tied quilts, using old blankets for batting and scraps of wool and corduroy for the tops. Quilts were also given to neighbors when homes burned. The Ladies Aid helped the community as a whole, not just church members.

Sarah Witte was the artist of the group. She was called upon when the group needed to come up with a quilting motif for a particular place on a quilt. She could cut a unique pattern to fit the space exactly. The box of patterns I received from my grandmother included templates made by Sarah Witte. Most of the templates are made of cardboard; empty cereal boxes, tablet backs, and old showbills were all put to service. On the back of some of the showbill templates you can still read the names of Betty Grable, Lauren Bacall, Audie Murphy, Marjorie Main, and John Wayne. The Mathieson General Store displayed the Pinconning Theatre showbills each

Figure 3. Cardboard templates made by Sarah Witte. Also purchased patterns ordered through the *Bay City Times*. (Photo by Debra Ballard.)

week. Louise Mathieson saved the old showbills which Sarah transformed into flowers, cables, birds, or whatever struck her fancy. The quilting designs were then marked by pencil on the quilt tops for the group to quilt.[12]

Any woman who wanted to quilt with the Ladies Aid could do so regardless of her quilting skills. One day a new quilter came to the group. She quilted all day, visiting with her friends and enjoying herself. After she left members discovered that instead of burying her knots in the batting when beginning each new thread, she had left each knot on the back of the quilt. Lydia Ehlers took the quilt home that night and ripped out all her friend's stitches, then requilted that portion of the quilt. The new quilter never knew about the extra work she had caused. At the next meeting she was gently shown how to bury her knots correctly in the batting. The group valued a person's feelings as much as high-quality quilting.[13]

Clara Rabe was well known for her excellent quilting. She also enjoyed talking while quilting. Louise Krevinghaus recalled, "Clara could almost sew as fast as talk." One day, Grandma Witte stood and watched her daughter, Clara, quilting and talking around the frame. Then, after a bit, Grandma Witte started laughing to herself. While talking, Clara had quilted over a large part of the quilt that was suppose to be quilted in a different pattern. Grandma Witte helped Clara take out the stitches and put in the planned quilting pattern.

All of the women made their own binding when it came time to finish the quilt. They usually trimmed the outside edge in either a contrasting color or a fabric used in the body of the quilt. They used either bias or straight-grain strips, depending on the amount of fabric they had on hand. Grandma Witte's customary first remark after putting a quilt in the frame was "What'll you bind it with?" Usually the binding was sewn on by machine, then turned over and hand-stitched to the back. Louise Mathieson does the opposite, though. She likes to see the small hand stitches on the front and feels it gives the quilt a finished look.

Quilting friendships and practices formed at the church also flourished in other settings. As a young boy, Dick Mathieson remembers marking quilt tops with a pencil for his mother, Louise. There was always a quilt set up in the Mathieson front room. The Mathiesons lived behind their general store in the village of Rhodes. Lena LaFrenier, Clara Rabe, and Ida Witte all lived in the village and would walk over to help quilt. All three older women were widows at the time. They enjoyed the companionship of quilting together in the pleasant afternoons, along with helping Louise, who was then a young wife with two boys. After quilting for awhile, the women would stop to wash dishes or even begin the evening meal while my grandmother worked in the store.[14]

I recall my summer visits at my grandparents' store. Like my father, I, too, experienced the chatter of the quilters coming from the front room. My own first quilting stitches were taken with both my great-grandmother and grandmother watching. There were long afternoons listening to the farmers swap stories with my grandfather or helping my grandmother in the store stocking shelves and waiting on customers. I loved to explore the attic and back bedrooms, discovering old pictures, high-top button shoes, and other miscellaneous knickknacks.

Figure 4. Mathieson's General Store served as a source for fabrics and notions. (Photo ca. 1940.) John Mathieson, who operated the store from 1918 until 1967, is standing in the center of the picture. Note the quilt on the horse. (Photo courtesy of Louise Mathieson.)

The years have brought changes to the community of Rhodes and the Ladies Aid. The people now find work in the cities and not on the farm. Mathieson's store has been gone for many years. People can easily travel the forty miles to the mall for whatever they need or want. Now only about eight members regularly attend the monthly meetings of the Ladies Aid. Most of these members have belonged to the church since the 1920s and 1930s. With women now working outside the home, the younger women do not find the time to participate in the Ladies Aid.

The Ladies Aid provided a focus for both the church and community of Rhodes, Michigan. But most importantly, the Ladies Aid provided an opportunity for friends and extended family members to come together for friendship, sharing, and support. That friendship and support extended into all aspects of community life, and its influence passed from one generation of women to the next. It is still at work in the Hope Lutheran Church today — a half century after it began.

Notes and References

1. Sandy Friedle, comp., *History of Hope Lutheran Church* (Rhodes, MI: 1989), 1.
2. Louise Mathieson, interview with author, December 23, 1988, Rhodes, MI, tape recording.
3. Lillian Meyer, interview with author, December 23, 1988, Pinconning, MI, tape recording.
4. Theresa Lindhurst, interview with author, January 25, 1989, Rhodes, MI, tape recording.
5. Paul and Minnie Witte, interview with author, January 28, 1989, Mason, MI, tape recording.
6. Minutes of Ladies Aid, 1940–1963, vol. 1.
7. Ibid., vol. 4.
8. Emma Rabe, interview with author, June 26, 1989, Pinconning, MI, tape recording.
9. Minutes of Ladies Aid, 1940–1963.
10. Louise Mathieson, interview with author, December 23, 1988, Rhodes, MI, tape recording.
11. Joyce B. Peaden, "Donated Quilts Warmed Wartorn Europe," in *Uncoverings 1988*, ed. Laurel Horton (San Francisco: American Quilt Study Group, 1989), 29–44.
12. Louise Mathieson, interview with author, December 23, 1988, Rhodes, MI, tape recording.
13. Louise Krevinghaus, interview with author, January 25, 1989, Rhodes, MI, tape recording.
14. Dick Mathieson, interview with author, December 27, 1988, Midland, MI, tape recording.

Quilts for Milady's Boudoir

Virginia Gunn

In 1925, France hosted *L'Exposition des Arts Decoratifs et Industriels Modernes*. This Paris exhibition celebrated several decades of development of what was then called "art moderne." Americans later shortened the fair's title and referred to this style of design as "art deco." The French invited the United States to participate in this international fair, but President Herbert Hoover declined, instead sending a large delegation to attend the event and report back to a three-man commission.[1] Hoover, as well as leading artists and designers like Paul Theodore Frankl, believed that American taste was almost exclusively for antiques or reproductions and that the United States "had no modern decorative art . . . not even a serious movement in this direction."[2]

This study shows that, contrary to this opinion, a movement in the direction of modern decorative art had begun at the grassroots or popular culture level shortly after it first appeared in Europe. Florence I. Goodenough, writing for the influential magazine *Arts and Decoration* in 1914, believed that Americans were "fast accepting this influence from the other side" in their "interior decorations, costume designs, and advertising."[3] An analysis of information collected from representative needlework, fashion, and decorating magazines serving American women between 1900 and 1940 and an examination of extant needlework made during this period supports her opinion.[4] Long before 1925, American women had adopted "art deco" or "art moderne" European fashion and design trends, incorporating them particularly into clothing and furnishings for the most intimate room of the house—the bedroom.

Virginia Gunn, Associate Professor, School of Home Economics and Family Ecology, University of Akron, Akron OH 44325.

In the first quarter of the twentieth century American women lavished attention, both "imagination and resource," on the decoration of their bedrooms.[5] The bedroom became more widely used as central heating made it a comfortable place to achieve a private niche in a smaller home. As increasing numbers of men went daily to work in offices and factories, they left women entirely in charge of decorating the domestic sphere. Women responded to advertisements telling them, "You spend more of your life in your bedroom than in any other room. It is logical to make that room—the first you see in the morning and last you see at night—as artistic and restful as you can."[6] The aesthetic choices women made influenced the design of quilts and spreads used in these settings.

As American women tired of Victorian bedroom decor, they often turned to "colonial revival" schemes.[7] Once again women became interested in traditional pieced and appliqued quilts. By 1905 *Harper's Bazar* reported that the American woman had "made herself acquainted with the lives of her colonial and Revolutionary ancestors" and had decided that the handicraft of her grandmother had "sufficient artistic value to allow it to demand an honored place in modern homes."[8] This interest helped fuel what Cuesta Benberry identified as the "20th century's first quilt revival."[9]

While nostalgic colonial motifs gained momentum, American women also continued their long-standing interest in the world of European fashion. As Europeans embraced modern art ideas, including an interest in boudoir effects, American women responded to these fashionable changes. They incorporated numerous French fashion influences into quilts made in the early twentieth century. Women did use antique quilts and they reproduced traditional designs. However, they also updated quilting, patchwork, and applique inspired by the "good old colony times" in a way that made it appropriate for what came to be called "milady's boudoir." They made or purchased large numbers of silk or rayon quilts, puffs, or comforts, and a variety of cushions, felt to be especially appropriate for a lady's boudoir. They used new colors and materials in their interpretations of older designs. They also created quilts with "art deco" or "art moderne" motifs. A number of quilts and spreads have an interesting juxtaposition of both colonial and boudoir influences, creating what may be called for want of a better term "colonial-boudoir" quilts or spreads.

This study explores ways American women used the colonial revival emphasis, which at first glance looks like a rejection of modern ideas, as a strategy to rationalize the adoption of new French fashion and furnishings for the most intimate room of the house, the bedroom. This strategy is poetically captured by Constance Vivian Frazier:

> Polly's quilting, now, they say
> In the easy, modern way.
> Rainy evening, radio,
> No special place to go;
> Polly lounges by the fire
> While the copper flames leap higher,
> And quilts a silken cushion fine
> In a pleasing new design.
> Nary quilting-frame has she —
> Holds her work on silken knee —
> But runs the minute stitches through,
> The way great-grandma used to do.
> Soft fingers touch across the years
> Above their quilting, it appears.[10]

French Boudoir Fashions

In the first decade of the twentieth century, the French, usually leaders in matters of decoration and artistic taste, had bogged down in Louis XVI revival decoration, after art nouveau had run its course. Paris had been somewhat slow to adopt the new and modern decorative ideas coming out of the workshops in Austria and Germany.[11] However, the opening of Sergei Diaghilev's *Ballets Russes* in Paris in 1909, and important exhibitions of modern furnishings at the 1910 *Salon d'Automne* and at the 1911 *Salon des Artists Decorateurs* turned the attention of French, once again, toward modern ideas in decorative arts and furnishings.[12]

The Russian Ballet's production of the oriental ballet *Scheherazade*, which opened in June 1910, fanned the fire of new ideas. The colorful Persian harem setting and sensuous dance costumes created an immediate sensation and launched a *Ballets Russes* style of fashion and decorating. Paul Poiret, a leading couturier, adapted Leon Bakst's costume ideas to women's fashions. Poiret also opened an interior decorating firm, the Martine Atelier, and created the type of interior boudoir settings these new clothes demanded. His designs started a vogue for clothes and bedroom accessories that had an interesting mix of oriental harem, Grecian, and French empire influences. Tasseled harem cushions decorated chaise longues (alias Grecian clines) and created the perfect background for the women clad in Poiret's slim unstructured low-necked empire or tunic gowns and turban headdresses.[13]

Fashionable American women had always followed French leadership. They immediately read of these scandalous and languorous styles of clothing and furnishings. Lady Duff-Gordon, or "Lucile" as she was known in the design world, described them for the readers of *Good Housekeeping*. She reported Parisian ballgowns made of the "flimsiest, coolest materials, and the lightest colors." She further noted that when the wearers of such fashions returned home from the dance they found "laid out for them the daintiest of night wear, and a boudoir wrap of soft gauze, encrusted with lace, in which to rest for a few minutes as they sip the cold soup that has been left for them by a thoughtful maid."[14]

American women not only began to think of such fashions, but actually to wear them. In 1913 Duff-Gordon commented on the fact that Ohio had passed laws prohibiting "transparent corsages, and low necks, and the slightest display of ankle." She told the "dear ladies of Ohio, you'll be sent straight to jail if you so much as walk a yard in your streets in 'la mode Parisienne' of to-day. I have not one word of hope for you."[15] Duff-Gordon went on to describe a dress of flesh-colored peau de soie and chiffon that gave the appearance of an unclothed body from a distance. She did not advise anyone, even outside of Ohio, to wear it in any public place.

The safest place to wear the more extreme French fashions was in the privacy of one's bedroom. American women had always prized French hand-embroidered lingerie and if unable to purchase these expensive articles at home or abroad, could possess such garments by embroidering them themselves.[16] American women who wished "to be truly in vogue" now began to purchase or make the more revealing lingerie, set off by boudoir caps, resembling the turbans of Poiret's fashions.[17] Inez Fox, writing for *The Modern Priscilla* in 1911, advocated loose boudoir jackets with large flowing sleeves that left the neck and arms "practically bare." She believed that "garments adapted for wear only in the privacy of one's own apartment, or, at best, within the limits of the family circle, afford the best opportunity for the display of fluffy, embroidered lingerie house sacks and gowns." She further felt that there were "very few women whose charms are not best displayed when the material of the gown is soft and clinging."[18] By 1914 *Needlecraft* editors informed readers that "it is the fashion of the day to wear pretty boudoir-caps and negligee gowns in the morning whenever possible. These are very 'homy,' and leave a pleasing impression on the mind of the men of the family who must leave us for the day.'"[19]

In 1916, *Needlecraft* editors reported that "the light and dainty effects" characteristic of French embroidered lingerie were now being incorporated into lingerie made by American women or manufacturers.[20] The Lever Brothers 1920 advertisement for Lux featured the maid Marie showing the lady of the house how to wash her new "soft crepe de Chine nightgowns, chemises of satin and lacy sheerness" so that she would not ever again be forced to wear the old "humble, horrible, 'other kind.'"[21] (Figure 1.)

Needlework and fashion magazines read by American women from 1910 to 1940 show an interesting juxtaposition of colonial and modern influences in both advertising and editorial sections. For example, *Vogue*, a leading fashion magazine, actually had a colonial lady, designed by the artist/illustrator Frank X. Leyendecker as their official trademark.[22] She appeared frequently on *Vogue* covers and at first glance, contrasts with cover designs featuring contemporary fashions.[23] However, her *polonaise* skirt, in Marie Antoinette dairymaid style, hovers above her ankles, and the low neckline of her colonial bodice is fairly revealing. She seems, on second thought, to contrast more with Victorian and Edwardian styles than contemporary ones. Readers could conclude that one's Victorian mother might object to new twentieth-century styles, but surely one's colonial great-grandmother would understand. She even went to sleep in her low-necked chemise with a mop night cap on her head, styles

Figure 1. A 1921 Lever Brothers' advertisement for Lux clearly shows the French-style boudoir fashions and furnishings illustrators presented regularly to American readers.

not that different from the new low-necked empire or kimono nightgowns with matching lingerie or boudoir caps. (Figure 2.) *Vogue* declared that their nostalgic trademark typified the distinctive spirit of fashion.[24]

Boudoir Settings

As women adopted French boudoir fashions, they began to feel the need for appropriate settings—light and dainty French bedrooms or boudoirs. *Webster's New Collegiate Dictionary* defines a boudoir as a small private room, especially one belonging to a lady. Elsie de Wolfe, author of *The House in Good Taste*, and one of the most influential decorators of the World War I era, believed that large American bedroom spaces should be divided to provide the "ideal arrangement" of an antechamber leading to a boudoir or sitting room, and then to a bedroom with a dressing room and bath.[25] American

Figure 2. January 1, 1917 cover of *Vogue* featuring a woman in her negligee and boudoir cap. The picture contains a mixture of colonial and modern art images very typical of this period.

Figure 3. A boudoir corner photographed for the April 1932 issue of *Arts and Decoration*. The Louis XV-style chaise longue is covered with a lace-edged cover made by Carlin Comforts.

middle-class women seemed to have neither the means nor the desire to go to such drastic measures. They continued to share their large bedrooms with their husbands, while modifying some of Wolfe's ideas to adapt the rooms to their new needs.

Women began to follow suggestions urging that they "invest a chamber, the boudoir of a woman, that most intimate of places, with a fine sentiment, that the occupant shall feel as if living in a suggested story."[26] Some women began to turn their bedrooms, "the most intimate, friendly part of the whole house," into feminine boudoirs.[27] After all, they had previously decorated corners of their parlors as exotic oriental cozy-corners during the Victorian era. Now a bedroom could be made to look like a Poiret-style boudoir/bedroom by providing it with a chaise longue or day bed covered with an appropriate boudoir quilt or comfort and the requisite number of tasseled and embroidered soft boudoir cushions. (Figure 3.) Advertisements began to include "the dainty little Settee of graceful lines, and heaped high with down cushions" in illustrations of the "ideal sleeping chamber."[28] When World War I made it difficult to import day beds and chaise longues, American entrepreneurs, aware of the new fad, began to manufacture "'occasional' models ... adapted from the antique to suit modern needs."[29] These included upholstered and reed versions of the chaise longue. Women who had no room for a day bed simply decorated their beds in boudoir fashion.

Boudoir quilts, comforts, or puffs could be either hand-quilted, machine-quilted, or tied. The best hand-quilted comforts featured luxurious or soft outer fabrics like velvet, satin, taffeta, or crepe de Chine and had warm lightweight fillings of lamb's wool or down. Quilt edges could be plain or scalloped, and trimmed with lace, ruffles, ribbon, or silk tassels. American women preferred plain colors, especially the "boudoir shades—flesh, peach, apricot, pink, blue, and orchid."[30] By the late 1930s darker colors like wine, deep blue, dark green, and gold replaced the "peach, French blue, eggshell, green, rose champagne, rose beige, and yellow" colors favored earlier in the decade.[31] A bedroom equipped with such comforters had an "aura of luxury" and offered a place to "luxuriate in quilted loveliness" according to needlework authorities.[32]

Cottage industries began to make the fashionable new boudoir quilts and to market them through leading periodicals such as *Harper's Bazar*, *House Beautiful*, and *Arts and Decoration*.[33] The Wilkinson Sisters, Ona and Rosalie, of Ligonier, Indiana, claimed to be "America's original makers of fine quilts."[34] They offered "art quilts" and "couch throws" and eventually marketed not only through catalogs and magazines, but through their seasonal shops in Palm Beach, French Lick, and Pasadena. They made quilts for the luxury market. The quilts, made entirely by hand in soft silks, satins, and sateens, had fillings of lamb's wool, cotton, or down. In 1917, they ranged in price from $10.00 to $150.00 depending on choice of materials, size, and design.[35]

Like other successful entrepreneurs the Wilkinson sisters used colonial strategies to promote their new projects, choosing names like Colonial and Queen Anne for some of their whole-cloth patterns considered "well-worthy for a Queen's boudoir."[36] Their adaptations of colonial whole-cloth designs often featured sytlish scalloped edges and included several patterns particularly suitable for hand-worked monograms, a characteristic feature of French-style lingerie. An editor of *Vogue* suggested that "a satisfactory method of hiding one's sorrows would be to slip under" such a cover and "leave no visible sign of one's identity but a beautifully embroidered monogram in the center."[37]

Carlin Comforts specialized in exquisite "accessories for the bedroom and boudoir," selling through their own shop in New York City and other smart stores such as Saks Fifth Avenue, I. Magnin, Neiman-Marcus, Joseph Horne, Julius Garfinkel, and the Edward Malley Company. Carlin products included "alluring feminine comforters and 'chaise-longue covers' in velvet and satin," and "dainty lace and satin covered pillows."[38]

Eleanor Beard had a studio in Hardinsburg, Kentucky, and outlets in major cities including New York City, Chicago, Pasadena, Santa Barbara, and San Francisco. Beard, a leading quilt entrepreneur in the 1920s and 1930s, sold old patchwork quilts but was best known for her own original designs executed by "skilled Kentucky needlewomen."[39] She sold every variety of "charming things to wear and for the boudoir," including monogrammed blanket covers, matching poufs and pillows, baby coach sets, taffeta travel throws, and appliqued quilts in contemporary designs.[40] Before the stock

Figure 4. Illustration from the February 1928 issue of *The Modern Priscilla* showing a traditional patchwork pattern in a strong color combination serving as a chaise longue cover in a very modern boudoir corner.

market crash her French taffeta comforts, single-bed size, sold for $85.00. At the height of the depression in 1932, she offered a taffeta Spider Web comfort for only $22.50 and monogrammed spreads for $7.50 to $8.50.[41] *House Beautiful* editors found her luxurious and "beautiful bits of feminine frippery . . . so refreshing in these days of pessimism."[42]

As the depression significantly reduced the purchasing powers of hundreds of Americans, established entrepreneurs and new manufacturing firms worked to provide the fashionable quilts and puffs at lower prices. Palmer Brothers Company of New York City offered "hand-guided patterns" for their comfortables of rayon taffeta or satin. They could provide down-filled comfortables for less than $16.00 or up to $22.50.[43] The Burton-Dixie Company of Chicago advertised an "Izolin down comforter" covered with Celanese taffeta for $19.95.[44] Would-be purchasers probably still found these prices somewhat steep in hard times. Some may have justified the purchase with the thought that sleeping under down would allow them to lower the heat in their homes without suffering.

In the 1930s and early 1940s silk whole-cloth boudoir quilts were often called trousseau quilts. Entrepreneurs and editors suggested that these silk-like quilts or puffs would make wonderful gifts for new brides.[45] The quilts came in sizes appropriate for both full beds and day beds. In difficult depression days chaise longues still seemed "very good for feminine morale. They make ladies who recline on them feel indolent and glamorous and wrapped in luxury, especially if the ladies are so fortunate as to have pillows and covers especially for their chaise longues."[46]

For women who wished to save money or express their own creative instincts, or both, needlework magazines and pattern companies provided designs for boudoir quilts, cushions, and accessories. In 1927, headlines in the McCall Company's quarterly needlework catalogue read "Early American Fashion for Quilting Restored Once More."[47] The company offered versions of the fashionable boudoir quilts and cushions in taffeta or radium silk. One scalloped-border art quilt had a stylized peacock quilted in the center, a motif also offered by the Eleanor Beard Studios. The illustrations feature maids holding up the quilts for the reader to view. A women could dream of such an atmosphere if she made and slept under one of these quilts.[48]

Modifying Traditional Patchwork

Not every woman wanted to switch entirely to whole-cloth silky boudoir quilts. Some chose to adapt traditional pieced and applique designs. Gertrude Schockey, writing for *The Modern Priscilla*, reported that "piecing silk coverlets for the day bed and the chaise longue is one of the most popular 'slants' of the quilting craze."[49] Pieced lace spreads used on French-style chaise longues or twin beds were offered "on the principle of the patchwork quilts which were the joy of an earlier generation."[50]

One of the easiest ways to adapt or update traditional patchwork was to copy the "fine old patterns" in new colors. The decorative art movement in Europe favored bright and intense colors. Some women copied traditional designs in vivid new color combinations or "startling black and white," a favorite of the Wiener Werkstaette in Vienna.[51] (Figure 4.) However, most American women with a "passion" for antiques favored more subdued or pastel colors.[52] They began to believe that "in our modern houses with smaller, heated bedrooms, we find soft pink or blues, cool greens or lavenders, or gay yellows combined with the mellow tint of unbleached cotton much better" than the stronger color combinations associated with European art deco or the nineteenth century quilts originally used or reproduced for colonial revival bedrooms.[53] Women began to use the favored boudoir colors in their more traditional work. Even conservative quiltmakers sometimes agreed that "when 'something old' had become 'something new' again, this 'something new' is never an exact reproduction of the old."[54]

Art Modern Designs for Traditional Patchwork

Another important way to update "colonial" patchwork involved using "simplified designs taken from genuine old bed quilts," or new designs related to the honored past.[55] American needlework designers had always worked to provide the readers of monthly women's and needlework periodicals with the latest in European designs. In 1910, *Home Needlework Magazine* reported that the "designers of patterns for embroidery can scarcely keep up with the demand for new ideas and artistic variations upon the old ones."[56] American women loved to embroider and looked for new ideas to replace Victorian, art nouveau, and arts and crafts designs. They wanted designs that would fit in with their preference for colonial revival. Early twentieth-century European designs fit this demand. By 1910, popular motifs coming from Germany, Austria, Italy, and France included modern versions of traditional motifs that ordinary people felt comfortable with.[57]

German designs in Biedermeier empire style and French rococo or empire designs had wide appeal. The German Biedermeier adaptations and reproductions had a classic quality. They featured such items as "odd stiff tubs and baskets of flowers, and apples, garlands and wreaths in which often appears the silhouette of some fair maiden of perhaps a hundred years ago."[58] French rococo revival designs featured stylized flower baskets trimmed with ribbons and garlands and wreaths or garlands of small flowers festooned with bow-knots.[59] This European repertoire of design motifs appealed to American women who applied them to quilting as well as embroidery. While these designs were "strictly up to date" they carried "the quaint, 'old-timey' atmosphere reminiscent of days Colonial."[60]

In the United States, people applied the adjective colonial to everything "from the earliest possessions of the Pilgrims to the designs in vogue as late as 1820."[61] Stylized flower baskets became reinterpreted as romantic "old-fashioned baskets" or "colonial baskets." Biedermeier silhouettes became colonial ladies "quaint in the dress of our great grandmothers."[62] Kate Mann Franklin argued in the *The Modern Priscilla*:

> Why should we always slavishly copy our grandmothers' quilting patterns? Surely our twentieth century designer has as good a knowledge of color, a better understanding of our modern aversion to 'plain sewing,' and a whimsical and charming imagination which she dares to use even when working with so humble a medium as cotton cloth."[63]

Well-known American needlework designers like Sophie T. LaCroix, Ann Orr, and Cora and Hugo Kirchmaier produced very appealing versions of these European designs in the second decade of the twentieth century.[64] Their cross-stitch designs feature wreaths, garlands, ribbons, baskets of flowers, butterflies, and small bouquets of stylized posies in the favored boudoir shades of yellow, blue, rose, green, and lavender. LaCroix and Orr later designed quilts incorporating these same color combinations and design motifs. Anne Orr Studios in Nashville, Tennessee, sold both completed quilts and kits.[65]

Marie Webster's influential book *Quilts: Their Story and How to Make Them* undoubtedly helped American women develop an early appreciation for stylized modern interpretations of traditional designs. The colored Bedtime Quilt in this book has a quilted border motif of Biedermeier-style topiary trees in tubs. Nine other colored plates display "modern" or conventionalized interpretations of flowers.[66] *The Ladies' Home Journal* for February 1918 featured Marie Webster's appliqued flower basket quilt, which would later be called the French Basket quilt.[67] This quilt appears on the same page with a Rose-Tree appliqued quilt, a flounced-edge silk couch cover, and two tassel-trimmed lounge or automobile throws. These offerings show the variety of alternatives available to women who wanted to be up-to-date in quiltmaking. In the 1920s, the Practical Patchwork Company of Marion, Indiana, marketed designs by Webster in either stamped or pre-basted kits.[68]

Colonial or Boudoir Sets

Some women preferred to decorate their bedroom/boudoirs with accessories that took less time to produce than patchwork quilts. By 1920, embroidered or embroidered-applique bedroom sets, called "boudoir sets" or "colonial sets," gained wide popularity. These practical, washable, and inexpensive sets were said to "add charm and character to a room which might otherwise be most uninteresting."[69] They consisted of matching bed-spreads, pillow-shams or pillows, window curtains, and dresser, bureau, table, or vanity covers all co-ordinated in favored colonial/art deco designs. Helen Grant imagined the "rosy dreams one who is fortuante enough to sleep in a room thus fitted up would be sure to have!"[70] The most fashionable and favored designs for these sets included flower baskets, old-time bouquets or nose-gays, and colonial ladies.

If this amount of embroidery or applique seemed a bit much, women could purchase a colonial girl kit complete with cardboard foundation and face to be decorated with bits of lace and pastel ribbon arranged to form a girl wearing a frilly dress of tiered ruffles and carrying an old-fashioned bouquet.[71] This concoction could then be mounted in the kit's decorative frame and hung in a place of honor on the bedroom or boudoir wall. In the 1940s, a framed colonial girl might still hang in a bedroom as a symbolic reminder of a time when modern girls embraced the future without completely forfeiting all old-fashioned values and virtues.

Summary

In 1914, Florence I. Goodenough predicted that the United States might "strike a proper adjustment" with the Modern Art Movement and "adapt it in a manner in harmony with her own people and her own temperament."[72] This study certainly suggests that this happened. From 1910 to 1940 American women used "colonial revival" as a strategy for embracing "moderne" ideas, rather than using it strictly as a nostalgic alternative to Victorian decoration and beliefs. The mixed modern and traditional images and messages found in advertising, editorials, and needlework can be interpreted as a strategy for cultural change. This strategy affected the fabrication and use of quilts. Using "colonial" rationalization, American women adopted revealing French lingerie styles and began calling their bedrooms "boudoirs." They purchased or created a variety of "colonial-boudoir" quilts, spreads, accessories, and decorations. These artifacts, which show direct influence of European decorative trends, remain as material culture symbols reflecting American women's intentional movement away from Victorian ideals and values and toward modern lifestyles and ideas they found more appropriate for the twentieth century.

Notes and References

1. Leslie Pina, "Louis Rorimer: Interior Design, 1896–1939," *Winterthur Portfolio* (Winter 1988): 243–64, esp. 261–62.
2. Martin Battersby, "The Triumph of Style: Art Deco," in *The History of Furniture* (New York: Crescent Books, 1976), 269–91, esp. 279–80.
3. Florence I. Goodenough, "The Modern Art Movement: How We May Apply the Movement Which Has Reached Its Highest Development in Germany," *Arts and Decoration* (September 1914): 420–21.
4. The magazines surveyed for this study include: *Arts and Decoration* (1913–1932), *Good Housekeeping* (1905–1913), *Home Needlework Magazine* (1899–1916), *House Beautiful* (1926–1940), *Needlecraft* (1911–1941), and selected issues of *Harper's Bazar* (1905–1923), *Ladies' Home Journal* (1895–1920), *The Modern Priscilla* (1905–1930), *Vogue* (1910–1930), and *Woman's Home Companion* (1915–1925).
5. Jane W. Guthrie, "Old Fashioned Counterpanes," *Harper's Bazar* (August 1905): 776–79, esp. 776.
6. "Above All—Your Bedroom," advertisement for Klearflax Linen Rug Co. in *Vogue* (February 1, 1917): 91.
7. B. Russell Herts, "The Historic Periods in Modern Households," *Arts*

and Decoration (September 1915): 432-35; A. T. Covell, "The Heritage of Historic Style: A Brief for Period Decoration," *Arts and Decoration* (September 1918): 283-85, 294.

8. Guthrie, 776. See also Jeannette Lasansky, "The Colonial Revival and Quilts," in *Pieced By Mother Symposium Papers*, ed. Jeanette Lasansky (Lewisburg, PA: Oral Traditions Project, 1988), 97-106.
9. Cuesta Benberry, "The 20th Century's First Quilt Revival," (3 parts), *Quilter's Newsletter* (July/August, September, October 1979): 20-22, 25-26 and 29, 10-11.
10. Constance Vivien Frazier, [Untitled Poem], *Needlecraft Magazine* (November 1928): 6.
11. Peter Quint, "The New Furniture of France, The Tenth Salon des Artistes Decorateurs," *Arts and Decoration* (August 1919): 186-87; Edward H. Ascherman, "New European Ideas of Interior Decoration," *Arts and Decoration* (June 1913): 279-81, 290.
12. Battersby, 273; C. Matlack Price, "Decoration and Color: A Discussion of Two Co-Existent Theories," *Arts and Decoration* (February 1915): 136-38.
13. Alain Leisieutre, *The Spirit and Splendor of Art Deco* (New York: Padding Press, Two Continents Publishing Group, 1974), 15-19, 163-95; see also Boris Kochno, *Diaghilev and the Ballets Russes* (New York: Harper & Row, 1970).
14. Lady Duff-Gordon ("Lucile"), "The Witchery of a Parisian Night," *Good Housekeeping* (October 1912): 521-23, esp. 523.
15. Lady Duff-Gordon ("Lucile"), "The Startling Styles of the Moment," *Good Housekeeping* (July 1913): 97-99, esp. 98.
16. "Embroidery Designs for Dainty Lingerie," in *Embroidery Lessons With Colored Studies, 1906* (New London, CT: Brainerd & Armstrong, 1905), 123-27.
17. "Boudoir Caps," *The Modern Priscilla* (March 1912): 29.
18. Inez Fox, "A Charming Negligee or House Jacket," *The Modern Priscilla* (October 1911): 33.
19. "Ladies Negligee and Cap," *Needlecraft* (December 1914): 24.
20. Kathryn Dubois, "A Dainty Set of Lingerie," *Needlecraft* (October 1916): 7.
21. "How to Keep Your Silk Underwear and Stockings," advertisement for Lux by Lever Bros. in *Woman's Home Companion* (March 1920).
22. "Spring Millinery Number of Vogue," advertisement for *Vogue* in *Life* (March 23, 1911): 602-3.
23. See excellent examples in William Parker, *The Art of Vogue Covers, 1909-1940* (New York: Harmony Books, 1980).

24. *Vogue* advertisement in *Life* (March 23, 1911).
25. Elsie de Wolfe, "Our House Interiors IX.—The Equipment of the Bedroom" *Good Housekeeping* (January 1913): 63-67, esp. 64.
26. Robert Tittle McKee, "Sentiment in Chambers: The Morning Glory Bedroom and 'Le Bouquet,'" *Good Housekeeping* (February 1905): 178-83.
27. Minna Hackett, "Bedroom Embroideries, Easy to Do and Extremely Good-Looking," *Needlecraft Magazine* (March 1928): 10-11.
28. "Hampton Furniture for the Country House Bedroom," advertisement for Hampton Shops of New York in *Vogue* (April 1, 1915): 101.
29. See editorial note in *Arts and Decoration* (December 1915): 102. For examples, see reed day bed in advertisement for The Reed Shop, Inc. in *Arts and Decoration* (June 1916): 411, and glazed upholstery chaise longue by Muller Brothers in "Christmas Gits," *House Beautiful* (December 1926): 715.
30. "Window Shopping," *House Beautiful* (January 1929): 2.
31. "Window Shopping," *House Beautiful* (June 1936): 5; "Color is the Bedroom Story," and "Color Combines for Beds," *House Beautiful* (February 1939): 45-48.
32. Christine Ferry and Louise H. Chrimes, "Luxuriate in Quilted Loveliness," *Home Arts—Needlecraft* (November 1935): 6.
33. For further information see Cuesta Benberry, "Quilt Cottage Industries: A Chronicle," in *Uncoverings 1986*, ed. Sally Garoutte (Mill Valley, CA: American Quilt Study Group, 1987), 83-100.
34. "Wilkinson Art Quilts Hand Made," advertisement in *Harper's Bazar* (April 1929): 216. See also the booklet *The Wilkinson Art Quilt* (Ligonier, IN: The Wilkinson Sisters, n. d., ca. 1915-1920).
35. "Wilkinson Art Quilts," advertisement in *Harper's Bazar* (November 1917): 111.
36. Wilkinson Sisters catalog page illustrating Queen Anne pattern in Malley Collection scrapbook, School of Home Economics and Family Ecology, University of Akron, Akron, Ohio.
37. "For the Hours When Woman Neither Toils Nor Spins," *Vogue* (January 1, 1917): 67.
38. "Decorative Ideas for Summer Beds," advertisement for Carlin Comforts in *House Beautiful* (June 1936): 85; Elizabeth Lounsbery, "From the Smart Shops and Antique Galleries," *Arts & Decoration* (March 1932): 8.
39. "Hand Quilted Things," advertisement for Eleanor Beard Inc. in *House Beautiful* (July 1927): 6 and (October 1929): 368.

40. Ibid., and advertisement for Eleanor Beard Inc. in *House Beautiful* (January 1929): 6.
41. Advertisements for Eleanor Beard Inc. in *House Beautiful* (October 1928): 344; (March 1932): 157; and (October 1932): 190.
42. Mary Jackson Lee, "Window Shopping," *House Beautiful* (December 1931): 458–59.
43. "Get Drowsy and you'll sleep Healthy, Wealthy and Wise!" advertisement for The Palmer Brothers Co. in *House Beautiful* (May 1936): 102; "You'll sleep like a baby every night," advertisement for Palmer Comfortables in *House Beautiful* (October 1938): 124.
44. "The Finest Gift of All," colored advertisement for Burton-Dixie in *House Beautiful* (December 1937): 9. Burton-Dixie said their Izolin process "cleans—purifies—and vitalizes feathers and down."
45. See, for example: "This is Quilting," *Woman's Day* (October 1941): 19–23; "Blanket Coverage," in the Bride's Issue of *House Beautiful* (October 1936): 68–69.
46. "Window Shopping," *House Beautiful* (June 1936): 5.
47. *McCall Needlework and Decorative Arts*, Winter 1927–28 (New York: The McCall Company, 1927): 17. Radium is a lustrous plain weave silk or rayon fabric that is somewhat crisp, yet soft and drapable.
48. For other examples using the French-style maid in needlework illustrations, see *Designer Needlework Book*, 1, no. 5 (New York: The Designer Publishing Co., 1920).
49. Gertrude Shockey, "A Placid Old Art Invades Our Hurrying Age," *The Modern Priscilla* (February 1928): 9, 55. See also "The Rising Sun," advertisement by Withers of Kirk, Kentucky, for a satin "Modernistic pillow made from an Early American pattern of 1752," in *House Beautiful* (October 1928): 358.
50. *Vogue* (January 1, 1917): 55.
51. Shockey, 55. See also Edward H. Ascherman, "New European Ideas for Interior Decoration," *Arts and Decoration* (June 1913), 281.
52. E. H. and G. G. Ascherman, "The Modernist School of Interior Decoration," *Arts and Decoration* (June 1914): 300–303, 324, esp. 301.
53. Shockey, 9. See examples of traditional quilts in softer modern colors in "Lovely Patchwork Quilts of Long Ago—Colorful Designs of Romantic Origin," *The Needle Arts Book, Fall and Winter 1930* (Chicago: Woman's World Magazine Co., 1929), 24–25.
54. Ethelyn J. Guppy, "Applique Blocks for Quilts and Other Things," *The Modern Priscilla* (January 1923): 35.
55. Virginia Dibble, "'Bed-Quilt Applique': Smart Motifs of Great-Grandmother's Designing," *Woman's Home Companion* (August 1924): 85.

56. "New Conventional Flower Designs," *Home Needlework Magazine* (August/September 1910): 263-65, esp. 263.
57. Battersby, 274. See also C. Matlack Price, "The 'Primitive' Note in Furniture: Modern Developments of Early Motifs in Design and Decoration," *Arts and Decoration* (May 1915): 279-80.
58. Bessie Berry Grabowski, "Biedermeier Embroidery," *Home Needlecraft Magazine* (October 1906): 322-28, esp. 322. See also "Biedermeier Embroidery," in *Embroidery Lessons with Colored Studies*, 1908 (New London, CT: Brainerd & Armstrong, 1907), 44-51.
59. "French Ribbon Work," in *Embroideries and Their Stitches* (New York: Butterick, 1905), 48-51, 82.
60. Ethelyn J. Guppy, "The Favorite Basket Design in Applique," *Needlecraft Magazine* (March 1925): 16.
61. Virginia Robie, "Colonial Furniture," *The House Beautiful* (October 1902): 279-80.
62. For an early example, see *Arts and Decoration* (November 1915): 60.
63. Kate Mann Franklin, "Twentieth Century Patchwork Quilts," *The Modern Priscilla* (August 1926): 12, 47.
64. See for example: Hugo W. Kirchmaier, *Book of Filet Crochet and Cross Stitch – Book No. 6* (Toledo, OH: Cora Kirchmaier, 1919); Sophie T. LaCroix, *Cross Stitch Designs – Book No. 7* (St. Louis, MO: St. Louis Fancy Work Co., n. d., ca. 1915); and Anne Orr, *Filet Crochet (Second Book) Cross Stitch Designs – Book No. 14* (Nashville, TN: Anne Orr, 1918).
65. Sophie T. LaCroix, *Martha Washington Patch Work Quilt Book – Book No. 12* (St. Louis, MO: St. Louis Fancy Work Co., n. d.; "Window Shopping," *House Beautiful* (October 1932): 192-93 featuring a French Wreath quilt by Anne Orr; and "Anne Orr Quilts," advertisement for Anne Orr Studios in *House Beautiful* (June 1932): 426. The applique Forget-Me-Not quilt in this Orr ad has strong resemblence to the Wilkinson Sisters' Mock Forget-Me-Not quilt advertised in *Harper's Bazar* (October 1929): 198, and to Eleanor Beard's Garden of Flowers design advertised in *House Beautiful* (April 1931): 341.
66. Marie D. Webster, *Quilts: Their Story and How to Make Them* (1915; reprint New York: Doubleday, Page, & Company, 1926).
67. "Two Comforts You Will Always Need: The Coverlet and Cushion," *Ladies' Home Journal* (February 1918): 110.
68. "Quilt – Early American Style," advertisement by Evangeline J. Beshore, Practical Patchwork Company, in *House Beautiful* (May 1929): 600.

69. Bennie Hall, "New and Pretty Togs for Dresing Up the Home," *Needlecraft Magazine* (December 1924): 10.
70. Helen Grant, "Patches Gay in Every Way Make Your Bedroom Bright Each Day," *Needlecraft Magazine* (May 1923): 10.
71. Advertisement for "'Colonial' Girl Lace Picture" in *Needlecraft* (January 1932): 18.
72. Goodenough, 422.

The Body En(w)raptured
Contemporary Quilted Garments

Jane Przybysz

From the many different feminist theoretical perspectives that presently circulate in academia, I have chosen to re-view contemporary quilted garments and quilted garment style shows from a materialist feminist perspective.[1] Focusing on specific garments created for fashion shows sponsored by Fairfield Processing Corporation and Concord Fabrics, I aim to offer the reader a materialist feminist way of thinking about the possible meanings of any garment in any style show.

As a materialist feminist, my research methodology and interpretive strategies are informed by a particular set of assumptions. Unlike other kinds of feminists, I regard the differences that exist between men and women as primarily a product of culture. I do not believe that, because women are biologically equipped to carry a fetus, they are necessarily more nurturing, caring, peaceful, or "natural" than men. If women appear to exhibit more of these qualities than men, I attribute this not to biology, but to the material conditions and social relations that (re)produce "woman." I am thus concerned with understanding how and why cultural, economic, political, and social institutions create "women" and "men."

As a materialist feminist, I am suspicious of institutions that historically have been created by and served the interests of primarily white, affluent men, and I question the so-called "universality" of the values these institutions claim to represent. Within the context of existing social, economic, cultural, and political institutions, I—unlike the liberal feminist—am not out to prove I can be "just like a man." For me, what it means to "be a man" is as much a fiction

---

Jane Przybysz, Department of Performance Studies, New York University, 725 Broadway, New York NY 10003.

as what it means to "be a woman." And unlike the cultural feminist, I do not consider myself innately different from or in any way superior to men. My aim is to understand the ways society creates categories of people called "women" and "men," categories which ultimately seem to limit the human potential of persons of both sexes. As a materialist feminist, I work within existing organizations with a critical awareness both of the ways in which those organizations oppress women and men, and of the differences that exist among women and among men in terms of class, race, and sexuality.

At present there exists only one in-depth scholarly analysis of the contemporary quilt revival—Lorre Marie Weidlich's "Quilting Transformed: An Anthropological Approach to the Quilt Revival."[2] In this 1986 doctoral dissertation, Weidlich discusses how embellished clothing worn by women at quilt events functions symbolically as both uniform and costume. As uniform, Weidlich says "embellished clothing announces quilters' affiliation" with other quilters by "show[ing] the incorporation of that activity into their own physical being." As costume, embellished clothing "disguises certain roles" and "advertises others." The roles it disguises, according to Weidlich, are that of housewife, mother, and working person; instead, "embellished clothing reflects a less central (but perhaps more passionately pursued) role." Unfortunately, Weidlich presents no analysis of the roles that quilters are "passionately" pursuing with the garments they create; nor does she consider the different meanings embellished garments have when worn or displayed in different contexts both at the quilt events and in quilters' everyday lives.[3]

Issues of power, gender, class, and race that are marginal to Weidlich's study are central to a materialist feminist analysis of the meanings of contemporary quilted garments and style shows. When and why do corporations become interested in producing quilted garment fashion shows? How does corporate sponsorship of style shows affect how and why women create quilted garments? Why has the making of embellished garments emerged as and continued to be primarily a "female" art form? What are the differences among the women who design and create quilted garments, and how does one account for the fact that this activity seems to appeal to women across class boundaries? Why is it that many of the women who make embellished garments do not make quilts? How does one explain the fact that it is mostly white women who are designing and making quilted and embellished garments in America? And why has the making of embellished garments emerged in the context of the present quiltmaking revival and not, for example, during the quiltmaking revival that occurred in America during the first quarter of the twentieth century?

It is certainly possible to describe contemporary quilted garments as simply the product of women expressing their creativity, and to characterize embellished garment style shows as wonderful opportunities for women to promote their talents and have fun. Re-viewing these garments and shows from a materialist feminist perspective, however, requires us to take them more seriously. Given the time, creative and emotional energy, and material resources some women invest in designing and making quilted and embellished garments, I believe embellished garments and the contexts in which they are displayed warrant serious attention. And although many or most women who make quilted garments do not consider themselves feminists, it seems to me that the questions raised by a materialist feminist analysis of the garments and the contexts in which they are modeled might be of interest to non-feminists and feminists alike.

In the summer of 1988, I attended Quilt Expo Europa in Salzburg, Austria, and for the first time saw a quilted garment fashion show. Presented by Concord Fabrics, the show offered a retrospective viewing of garments created for the Fairfield/Concord Fashion Show which, since 1979, has premiered annually at the Houston Quilt Festival.[4] Also included in the show were garments made by European designers specifically for the event.

My response to the show was one of delight and confusion. As a quilter, I was awed by the design and technical virtuousity exhibited by the makers of these garments, and spellbound by the display of so many sumptuously colored, textured, and embellished fabrics. As a materialist feminist trying to decipher the meaning of these garments and of the fashion show as a whole, I was intrigued and troubled.

Many of the garments defied easy categorization as daytime or evening wear, as formal or informal wear, as indoor or outdoor attire, as junior, misses or women's wear. Several garments were made to be reversible. A *Flyfishing Woman's Evening Attire* consisted of sporty-looking, cotton appliqued pants and vest, thus straying far from and perhaps even parodying what most people would consider appropriate "evening attire." Were quilters playing with and disrupting the categories according to which we ordinarily dress and define who we are and how we should behave according to the time of day, place, gender, age, marital status, class and race? If so, it would seem that—for some women—making quilted and embellished garments might be a way of manipulating and resisting society's idea of what constitutes an ideal American woman.[5] Making embellished garments might be an act of rebellion, a form of political action. Indeed, when *God Save the Queen* by Kim Masopust turned out to be a floor-length, black velvet coat depicting Henry VIII and all his dead wives, I felt I was watching a moment of feminist theater.[6] Didn't Henry's wives die because they failed to perform their role as "wife" and produce a male heir to the throne?

The degree to which many of the garments seemed to avoid prescribing an ideal female body type was remarkable. Georgia Bonesteel's *That Cotton Pickin' Garment*, Vickie Martin's *Midnight Beauty*, and Bonnie Benson's *Jewel of India* were all unfitted, tunic-like garments that might accommodate any number of body sizes and shapes. And by refusing to reveal, to focus on, or fetishize any part of the female body (the breasts, the legs, the waist, the hips), all of these garments seemed to frustrate "the male gaze" that feminist film critics have identified as one of the mechanisms by which women come to act, not in their own interests, but in the interests of men.

In the 1970s, film scholar Laura Mulvey began looking at the way narrative films construct an ideal spectator.[7] Since the vast majority of films are shot by men with the eye of the camera simulating the point of view of the main character of the story who, in most cases, is male, she suggested that the ideal spectator constructed by most narrative films is male. She posited that "woman" in these films is positioned as "other" in relation to "man," and becomes that which is exchanged among the male characters in the film, and between the male hero of the film and the male spectator.

But what happens when women watch these films? On the one hand, the female spectator is obliged to identify with the male hero, in whose eyes "woman" is generally one of three things: the passive object of male sexual desire, the self-sacrificing helpmeet who helps man achieve his goals, or the obstacle to be vanquished. Because women are usually denied any active role in the film narrative itself, women watching these films are forced to identify with one of these three kinds of women. Understandably, most choose to identify with the object of male sexual desire or with the woman who erases herself for his benefit. Eventually, feminist film theorists argue, the female spectator comes to experience both these roles as pleasurable because of her identification with the male gaze of the hero. In other words, women watching narrative films internalize "the male gaze" and come to enjoy playing out the kinds of passive roles that make them desirable and attractive to men. Instead of perceiving and enjoying their "selves" in a subject position, capable of acting in and upon the world, women tend to perceive and enjoy their "selves" in an object position, in relation to "the male gaze."[8]

What was exciting about so many of the garments shown in Salzburg was that they seemed to potentially frustrate "the male gaze." By refusing to represent "woman" as a fetishized sex object or self-sacrificing helpmeet, many of the garments potentially disrupted white male-dominant cultural narratives. Finally, garments which were quilted and embellished in a way that invited close inspection threatened to collapse the physical distance that seems to make voyeurism possible.

But there were several things about the fashion show that troubled me. First, this was the only event at Quilt Expo Europa that was introduced by a man. George Gleitman, President of Concord's Home Sewing Division, delivered the opening remarks for the fashion show.[9]

Second, I was dubious of the comparison that Priscilla Miller, Sales Executive for Concord Fabrics and fashion show commentator, made between this fashion show and the tradition of the quilting bee. Early in the program she said, "Just as in the old-fashioned quilting bees, this has been a volunteer afternoon, and we have quite a cadre of young women from among you who have volunteered both to help backstage and to model." The idea of the quilting bee implies a collective enterprise in which everyone participates as equals. Each woman who joins in a quilting bee theoretically has the right to ask help from all the women she helps; there is a reciprocal relationship among the quilters. Miller's comment seemed to mask the uneven power relationship that exists between corporate sponsors of the show and the quilters whose volunteer labor (that invested in the design and making of the garments and that used to mount the show) made it possible.

Third, there were garments that looked as if they'd been made to activate a "male gaze." *Midsummer Night's Dream* by Ann Boyce, for example, looked as much like "his" dream as hers. An evening gown with a fitted, low-cut bodice and sleeves off the shoulder conspicuously displaying the breasts, neck, and shoulders, this garment seemed to fetishize the female body. Likewise, Kim Masopust's *Pavo Cristatus* (Latin for "peacock"), while covering the entire body, clung to the breasts and cinched the waist in a manner that emphasized the hourglass-like female figure that supposedly sends men aswooning.[10]

The way the garments were modeled and described also seemed, for the most part, to construct a male gaze and traditional male narratives in which women do not act as subjects of their own, but in accordance with the desires of men. What most people have come to know as the traditional fashion show format — the procenium stage with a runway jutting out into the audience — was disturbingly familiar, reminding me of the Miss America pageants I avidly watched until I realized that there was something peculiar about young women being awarded scholarships based on how they looked (to men? to women viewing from the point of view of the male gaze?) in bathing suits and evening gowns. Also, words like "feminine," "ladylike," and "to the moment" were used to characterize garments as if those terms were universally understood and valued.[11]

Finally, unlike the women attending the conference who came in all shapes, sizes, and ages, the women who volunteered or were asked to volunteer were mostly young and mostly slender. (It wasn't until later that I learned that all garments for the Concord/Fairfield Fashion Show must be made a size ten.) Moreover, watching this fashion show foregrounded for me the startling absence of women of color at this conference. Not one model was black, Hispanic, or Asian.[12]

Months later, when I began to prepare this essay, I contacted Debbie Driscoll at Fairfield Processing who was kind enough to loan me slides from three previous fashion shows, as well as the programs that listed the names of the garments and their makers. Looking over the programs, again it seemed as if the titles some women had given their garments indicated that fashion show participants aimed to represent "woman" as a desiring subject. Titles like *Hot Ice, Wild Thing, Dance Electric, Tropical Heat, Things That Go Bump in the Night, I Wanna Dance With Some Body, There'll Be a Hot Time in the Old Town Tonight,* and *Spacial Palatial Dancin'*... *The Black Hole Strut* seemed to construct "woman" as unrestrained, sensuous, moving to her own rhythms, her own desires. The "queen theme" was still there. And there were additional categories suggested by the titles.

A strong dream/fantasy motif ran through the different fashion show programs: *California Dreamin', Desert Moon Dream, Dreaming Down Under, Fantasia, Super Star Fantasy, Fan-see This.* Another group of titles seemed to express a similar metaphysical yearning for movement, for change, for another mode of being: *Vision Quest, Crystal Transformation, Extension, Cruising the Planet.*

But the way the garments were represented in the slides—by all-American-looking, white, young, size-ten women posed according to the conventions of fashion photography for the male gaze—neutralized to a large extent the challenge some of these garments might have presented, were they to have been photographed on or in the presence of the women who made them. In other words, the degree to which some of these garments might have functioned as a critique of dominant cultural constructions of "woman" as comforter, as wife, as mother, as America, had been all but erased by the way they were represented in the slides. The slides position the garments, position "woman" as the object of a male gaze.[13]

The garment I chose to consider in depth was Virginia Avery's *There'll Be a Hot Time in the Old Town Tonight,* as shown in a slide being modeled by a young professional model. Like many other quilters, I have a high professional and personal regard for Virginia Avery. I believed that, while she might not agree with my analysis of her work, she would welcome serious consideration of the work of women fiber artists like herself. In addition, the outfit is "problematic" is a way that is useful for the purpose of this essay.

Talking with Virginia Avery, I learned that the garments she designs allow her to "work through a creative idea," and the fashion shows are an opportunity to "compete with other artists and create something that will stand out and be indicative of my creativity and will command the respect of my peers." With the garment she entitled *There'll Be A Hot Time in the Old Town Tonight*, she "wanted something that looked a little bit sedate from the outside, but pretty racy from the inside. And I really thought of the flapper time . . . very short and flippy clothes . . . on women out for a good time, having a lot of fun."[14]

Were it not for being invited to participate in the Concord/Fairfield Fashion Show, Avery says she's not sure she'd be making these garments. Clearly, however, they function practically as a form of self-promotion. Since the fashion shows travel both nationally and internationally, Avery's name — already well known and respected amongst quilters — remains highly visible in the quilt community. After the garments tour, she will often use them as teaching tools in the workshops she gives. And if they are something she'd wear, well, then she might even wear the garment.

If they are something she'd wear? Why would she make something she wouldn't wear? Avery indicates that, in thinking about designing the garments she makes for style shows, her primary consideration is how they will look on the runway. She aims for a "good runway effect," a look that will be "striking" and "effective" from a distance. The relationship between the garment she creates, her body, and her "self" seems secondary, incidental.[15] When speaking about *There'll Be a Hot Time in the Old Town Tonight*, for example, she indicates that while she might choose to wear the coat, she wouldn't wear the flapper-like dress she ultimately created as part of the outfit she designed. It isn't "her."

> I'm too old for it. . . . I no longer wear things with just straps at the shoulders, and it's too short for me. I'm much more comfortable in a longer length. . . . My tastes have changed. I'm no longer comfortable in a sleeveless or strap dress or in a very short one. I wear pants almost all the time. I find pants so practical and so comfortable.

Without talking to Avery I would have assumed that *There'll Be a Hot Time in the Old Town* was an extension of her "self. And yet, it appears that this is not the case — that aesthetic considerations override Avery's concern with personal self-expression.

There'll Be A Hot Time in the Old Town Tonight is an outfit that consists of a black, sleeveless, knee-length sheath dress; a full-cut, quilted, ankle-length coat which is black on the outside and lined with panels of yellow, pink, purple and green; a multi-colored body ornament composed of squares of fabric, beads and tassels; and a multicolored evening pouch. The slide made available to me by Fairfield Processing Corporation represents *There'll Be a Hot Time in the Old Town Tonight* on the size ten body of a young, white, all-American-looking woman. She is posed according to the conventions of fashion photography, smiling, in heels, hips thrust slightly forward, her left knee bent and angled towards her right leg so that the profile of her calf is visible to the camera. It is a pose that seems to freeze her as the passive, anonymous, silent object of male desire. It is a pose that seems to construct me as a male spectator. How might one begin to interpret the possible meanings of this garment?

I try to imagine the garment without the model in the picture and ask: **What kind of body is being articulated?** There seem to be two. There is the straight, narrow-hipped, flat-chested body suggested by the sheath dress and there is another, less constrained, less clearly articulated body suggested by the coat and the body ornament, either of which looks as if it might accommodate any number of body types.

In an article entitled "Buying and Selling the LOOK," Kate Davy considers the way that garments historically have constructed ideal female body types.[16] She is especially concerned with those historical periods in which a slender, small-breasted, thin-hipped, boyish body type has been most fashionable: the last quarter of the nineteenth century when appearing "consumptive" was *la mode*; the roaring twenties that brought us the flapper look; and the 1960s, when the Twiggy look made its debut. Observing that boyish bodies seem to become fashionable when women have organized most successfully to promote social and political change, Davy suggests that this is perhaps no accident. Since most women do not "naturally" have this type of body, clothing that requires boyish figures encourages women to expend considerable time, energy, and money on diets, exercise programs, and sometimes even surgical procedures to make their bodies "fit." In extreme cases, women become bulimic or anorexic in their efforts to achieve the "look."

What better way to undermine women's presence as social and political actors in the public sphere than to promote a "look" that most women do not measure up to—or down to, as the case may be? If women with the time and economic means to work for political change can be kept perpetually dissatisfied with bodies—especially hips and thighs—that are never thin enough, and perpetually busy trying to achieve whatever look is being promoted as fashionable and attractive to men, it is unlikely they will find the time, energy, or self-esteem they need to be politically vocal or visible. Davy's article leaves one wondering: Is it just a coincidence that the Twiggy look became the rage in 1967, the year that the National Organization for Women was founded?

When I look at the sheath dress that is part of *There'll Be a Hot Time in the Old Town Tonight*, I note that it seems to prescribe the boyish body that most women don't have. The coat and body ornament, however, are not so prescriptive. The coat appears to have enormous raglan sleeves, no padding at the shoulders, and it flares towards the bottom. The body ornament is stitched in the fashion of coats of mail and looks as if it would conform to whatever shape it was slipped over.

The second question I ask myself when attempting to get at the possible meanings of a garment is: What kind of female subject does this outfit construct? Or, in other words: **What cultural narratives does this outfit suggest and what is "woman's" position in these narratives?** Again, I try to imagine the outfit apart from the model in the slide, because as soon as the garment is on a body, that body—its size, age, color, and the way it moves or is posed—largely shapes its meaning.

While it is difficult to recall my reading of this outfit before I interviewed Ms. Avery and before I read the article about the outfit she wrote for *Threads Magazine*,[17] my notes indicate that what struck me about this outfit was the way it juxtaposed, played with, and confused categories according to which we conventionally read clothing and read "woman." The different parts of the outfit seem to suggest different cultural narratives so that it becomes virtually impossible to attribute any one meaning to it.

For me, the narrative that the slip-dress suggests is that of a young professional woman at a cocktail party who wants to be taken seriously, yet to appear attractive to men. The dress flattens, straightens, and thereby desexualizes the torso, but displays the shoulders, arms, and legs. Her body is there for men to see, but not in a way that might be interpreted as sexually aggressive or threatening. The potential wearer of this garment might be intellectually challenging, but she presents herself as the passive object of male sexual desire.

Adding the body ornament, however, confuses this narrative. The bright, multi- and metallic-colored squares of fabric sewn on the diagonal like chain mail, further flatten the upper torso, seeming to guard yet draw attention to the chest. I am reminded of the multicolored jester's costume composed of colorful diamond shapes. The strings of beads, smaller cloth squares, and tassels that hang freely from the waist of the body ornament playfully tease and titillate. The body ornament appears to eroticize the torso but curiously makes it less available. The sheath dress causes the torso of the body to virtually disappear (black is the color all women wear to look thinner), but the body ornament brings it back to life. The woman who would wear this could hardly be described as the passive object of male sexual desire. As she moves the body ornament would brush against her body, tickling her at the same time as it teases the viewer's eye. The body ornament thus seems autoerotic as well as a means of inviting the male gaze.

Adding the coat further complicates the picture. It covers the shoulders, the arms and potentially even the legs. The silhouette created at the side seams of the large raglan sleeves and the body of the coat, as well as along the bottom of the coat, is reminiscent of the stylized Christmas trees all children draw. Gold coins stitched at each point of a would-be branch weight them down so that they appear more like prairie points than branches.[18]

What might this coat mean? Borrowing the image of a tree from nature, does this coat portray "woman" as nature or is it intended as a parody of "woman" as nature? Are the gold coins stitched to the outside of the coat intended as a kind of commentary upon the way in which, since the industrial revolution, middle- and upper-class women increasingly have assumed less productive roles in society and more a display function—displaying the wealth and status of their husbands upon whom they have become economically dependent?[19] Or does this garment collaborate with the body ornament to conjure the image of "woman" as jester? Certainly the pointed edges of the coat, and the brightly colored panels of fabric that comprise the lining are suggestive of jesters' costumes. Is Avery playing with the conventions of what is considered appropriate lining? Most contemporary coats are decoratively colored on the outside, and lined with a solid, neutral fabric. The coat in *There'll Be a Hot Time in the Old Town Tonight* is black on the outside and multi-colored on the inside.

In effect, the outfit seems to construct a female subject which is multiple and variable, depending on the way the different garments that make up the outift are worn. When all three pieces are worn together, they construct a "look," a "woman" who is not easy to peg according to conventional male narratives as "ingenue," "married housewife," or "working mother." The "woman" this garment constructs is not an unambiguous, passive object of male sexual desire, and she is clearly not the helpmeet type. More likely than not, this outfit is suggestive of the kind of "woman" the male hero of a film might perceive to be a obstacle; she seems controlled yet outspoken, sensuous, witty, self-possessed, and something of a rebel. In other words, she appears to have a mind and desires of her own.

Up to this point, I've tried to analyze *There'll Be a Hot Time in the Old Town Tonight* from a purely visual point of view apart from the body on which the outfit has been represented in the slide. Now I find it necessary to ask: **How does the title a quilt artist assigns an outfit inflect its meaning?**

As a musician who plays piano in a Dixieland jazz band, Avery often entitles the garments she makes with titles of popular songs, as she has done with *There'll Be a Hot Time in the Old Town Tonight*. The lyrics of many popular songs, especially older songs, unfortunately position "woman" as the passive object of male sexual desire. But the way Avery uses this title, seems to position "woman" as the speaker, as the person actively seeking a "hot time" later that evening. Overall, then, it seems as if *There'll Be a Hot Time in the Old Town Tonight* constructs a "woman" who negotiates two bodies — that which seeks the approval of the male gaze and that which experiences itself as having a mind and body with desires of their own. The result is an outfit that defies easy categorization, and that implicitly resists traditional male narratives in which woman represents either the object of male sexual desire or the eternal comforter — wife, mother, and America.

Yet any analysis of the possible meanings of contemporary quilted and embellished garments designed for style shows must consider: 1) **How do the rules for participating in the style show shape the kinds of garments quilt artists design and create?** and 2) **How does the way the garments are presented affect the way we read the meaning of the clothing?**

Invitations to participate in the Concord/Fairfield Processing Fashion Show go out every January, and the garments must be completed by August. Designers are not paid either for their work or for the rights to tour their garments both nationally and internationally for one year after the show's premiere in Houston. Many quilters, however, perceive the visibility that the show affords them as compensatory. Participating sponsors also make free materials and notions available to the designers.

There are only four guidelines for participating in the show.

(1) The designer must use Fairfield batting somewhere in the garment. This does not seem to limit quilters in any way since there are no criteria as to how much one has to use or where one uses it. This rule does insure, however, that every garment represents and promotes Fairfield Processing Corporation.

(2) Garments must be made a size ten. For women who do not make garments as extensions of their personal selves, but rather for the show, this does not pose a problem. Put another way, this rule seems to discourage women from thinking of these garments as expression of their "selves" and to encourage them to design garments for the show to achieve a good runway look. For designers who happen to wear size ten clothes and want to wear the garments they make, this rule makes no difference. But generally speaking, by prescribing an ideal body type that the bodies of most women do not match, this rule potentially alienates the quilt artist who is not a size ten from her own body, and discourages her from creating garments that play with or challenge that culturally constructed ideal.

Elinor Peace Bailey is one quilt artist who has found a creative solution to the problem posed by this rule.[20] After making her first garment for the style show a size ten—a size she herself cannot wear— she henceforth chose to use a T-dress pattern that can later be adapted for her to wear, and concentrated on quilting and embellishing a one-size-fits-all tabard to be worn over the dress. I wonder how many other women have been required to be similarly creative or to view the garment they make as something they create "for the show" and not for their "selves"?

It is easy to understand, from the point of view of corporate sponsors who hire professional models for the Houston show, why asking quilt artists to make size ten garments makes perfect sense. While there are now modeling agencies that represent larger women, most professional runway models wear size ten garments. Also, having garments be approximately the same size facilitates the process of selecting volunteers from local quilt guilds to model the garments in shows mounted after Houston. Yet given the negative body image most women have, it is equally easy to imagine how potentially self-alienating it might be for a woman to expend a tremendous amount of volunteer time, creative energy, and sometimes money to create a garment she cannot wear.[21]

(3) Style show participants must submit a complete outfit—not just a jacket or a skirt. From the point of view of corporate sponsors, as well as that of the quilt artists I've interviewed, this rule—like the size ten rule—makes perfect sense and is not perceived as a limitation. This way Fairfield ensures that the outfit modeled is the total "look" intended by the designer, not a collaboration between the designer and Fairfield Processing staff. If designers only submitted a jacket, for example, someone at Fairfield would be in the position of having to choose the pants, skirt, or dress over which the jacket would be modeled. I don't perceive this rule to be a limitation, except in instances where designers interpret "complete outfit" as "complete matching outfit." But, certainly, this rule did not prevent Avery from creating an outfit that gave off mixed messages and potentially disrupted conventional cultural narratives that position "woman" as either the passive object of male sexual desire or his self-sacrificing helpmeet.

(4) The quilter must title her garment. This is where quilt artists are given the opportunity to have a voice in how their garments will be represented and interpreted. Surveying the titles quilt artists give their garments indicate that this is indeed a venue for them to frame their garment as, in some sense, a cultural critique. Titles like *I Only Make Samplers* and *My Own Little Statement* used to characterize garments that are far from "humble" or "little" seem ironically to critique the notion that "woman" should be meek or

self-effacing. The many titles with references to "heat" and/or "dancing" seem to present an idea of "woman" as a sensuous, desiring subject, rather than the passive object of male sexual desire. Finally, the kinds of dreams and fantasies suggested by many of the titles bear little resemblance to the kinds of dreams and fantasies (of men, of marriage, of motherhood) that conventional cultural narratives portray women as having.

Quilted and embellished clothing—even outfits created for a specific style show—can have very different meanings in different contexts. Virginia Avery has made it very clear that she made *There'll Be a Hot Time in the Old Town Tonight*—not for herself, but to achieve a stunning runway look. But just as an exercise, suppose we imagine Avery waking up one Sunday morning and choosing to wear the outfit to church. Since most Christian doctrine—regardless of denomination—discourages women from experiencing their bodies, their "selves" as pleasurable outside the institutions of marriage and motherhood, many members of the congregation would be likely to find Avery's wearing *There'll Be a Hot Time in the Old Town Tonight* offensive. A materialist feminist, however, might read and applaud her action as a powerful statement about the rights of any woman, but especially an older woman, to express a desiring, sensuous, sexual self.

If Avery chose to have *There'll Be a Hot Time in the Old Town Tonight* modeled only in style shows mounted with non-professional models, the outfit might represent an opportunity for other women to "try on" or rehearse a sensuous, desiring "self" that the culture at large does not nurture. To the extent that life follows art, that we learn through imitation, through mimesis, *There'll Be a Hot Time in the Old Town Tonight* might serve as an agent for change in the bodies, the self-perceptions, and, ultimately, the lives of both the women who wear the outfit, and the women in the audience who imagine themselves wearing the outfit.

The Concord/Fairfield Fashion Show draws upon the conventions of commercial fashion shows, making use of a combined procenium/thrust stage with little or no ornamentation that might distract from or contextualize the garments shown. The fashion show narrator stands behind a podium in a position of authority with the only microphoned voice. Models appear from an invisible offstage space and parade silently in a manner intended to obscure their bodies, their selves, to insure that the garment remains the focus of attention. A largely silent audience observes from a distance.

While most people perceive the conventional fashion show format as "natural," it in fact encodes very definite hierarchical power relations and constructs the ideal spectator as "male." This became very apparent at Quilt Expo Europa when, immediately following the fashion show, other garments were modeled by their makers in a show and tell session. Approaching from the audience, quilters mounted the stage, used the microphone to give voice to information that contextualized the garment they wore, and then modeled the garment they made on their own bodies in a manner that—more often than not—could not be described as self-effacing. In the show and tell session, no longer were silent, self-effacing women modeling garments made by invisible authors being presented by a fashion show narrator for the viewing pleasure of the audience. Audience members were representing their garments and their "selves" for other audience members.

Producers of the Concord/Fairfield style show seem to be sensitive to these issues. At Quilt Expo Europa, fashion show commentator Priscilla Miller introduced many of the garments with biographical information about the quilt artists, sometimes quoting them directly. She introduced the volunteer models by name. Miller also wore a quilted garment which she had commissioned from one of the artists, which in some sense, made her "just one of us" instead of a corporate representative. Because the models had been festival participants, they were known by many in the audience and this seemed to mediate the voyeuristic distance and male gaze invoked by the procenium stage which constructs "woman" as the passive object of male desire.

The extent to which a style show depends on the conventions of theatrical representation used by commercial fashion shows, in large part, determines the extent to which any garment can propose or argue for social or political change. The more the male gaze and the hierarchical power relations generated by that representational frame are disrupted and/or foregrounded, the greater the possibility that "woman" can become culturally audible and visible as something other than the passive object of male desires.

Producers of the Fairfield/Concord show have traditionally organized garments in a given year's show according to some theme. The outfits in the 1986 show were grouped under headings inspired by the names of painters, headings like Mostly Monet, Really Renoir, and Mystical Miro.[22] In 1987 jewels were the common denominator among categories: Splendidly Sapphire, Traditionally Topaz, and Romantically Rose Quartz. The 1988 show was organized around the names of constellations: Creatively Corona Borealis, Comfortably Columbia, and Graphically Gemini. Beginning with the 1988 show, producers experimented with coordinating music with the various sections. The garment that opened the 1988 show—*Be a Sport!* by Jeanne DeWitt—was modeled to the theme song from the film "Rocky."

How do the themes chosen by style show producers affect how we interpret the garments we see? Grouping garments primarily according to how they will look together, Donna Wilder placed *There'll Be a Hot Time in the Old Town Tonight* in the category "Lively Lynx" along with *Sweet Sixteen* by Jean Wells Keenan and *Silk Trade—Thank you, Marco Polo!* by Carol Higley Lane. Would we have read Avery's outfit differently had it been grouped with other outfits according to the themes implied by the titles designers had given their creations? What if *There'll Be A Hot Time in the Old Town Tonight* appeared with *Things That Go Bump in the Night* by Charlotte Warr Anderson, *Wild Thing* by Gayle Earley, and *Dance Electric* by Susan Deal under a heading that read "Quilters Hot to Trot" or "Women on the Loose"? Does organizing shows around themes that do not seem to emerge from or be inspired by the titles designers give their garments neutralize or deflect attention away from the degree to which many of these outfits potentially critique conventional cultural ideas of "woman? Does grouping garments according to how they "look" together rather than according to themes suggested by garment titles privilege the aesthetic dimension of the garments at the expense of the social or political dimensions?

How does the music used to frame a garment affect its meaning? When the theme song from "Rocky" is played as *Be A Sport!* is modeled, how does the audience interpret that outfit? *Be A Sport!* consists of a pair of white polyester satin running shorts worn with an embellished, white satin warm-up jacket: and its title seems intended to be ironic. When someone says, "Be a sport," she generally means "Be a good loser" or "Make the best of a bad situation." With the garment she created, Jeanne DeWitt seems to be saying just the opposite: Don't Be A Good Sport! Don't settle for less than what you want! The garment implicitly critiques the idea that "woman" should be self-denying, self-effacing, or self-sacrificing.

On comes the theme song from "Rocky," a film about a mediocre club fighter who—given the opportunity—works to reach his potential. In the process, he effects a transformation upon the mouse of a pet shop clerk he woos from an unfashionably plain girl into a fashionably beautiful woman. When we hear this music and watch a young, white, conventionally pretty woman model a white satiny gym outfit, what do we see? Do we imagine that the model is the quilt artist who, like Rocky, is a person who, given the opportunity to participate in a style show—to become culturally visible—works to reach her potential? Do we see the professional model as the girlfriend, the fashionably beautiful woman Rocky makes of the ugly duckling pet store clerk? Or does the song just wash over us and make no difference whatever in how we read this outfit?

How might we interpret *Be A Sport!* if, instead of hearing the theme song from "Rocky," we listened to Helen Reddy singing, "If I have to, I can do anything. I am strong, I am invincible, I am WOMAN," from her song, "I Am Woman"? It seems that the music one chooses to represent an outfit or group of outfits potentially selects, amplifies, and/or mutes particular interpretations of an outfit.[23]

In 1989, Czechoslovakian-born artist Jana Sterbak created an imposing motorized skirt made of aluminum strips which she called *Remote Control I* to be modeled by a woman wearing a white leotard and tights in art museum contexts. The skirt can be operated by the woman wearing it. It can be programmed to move independently of whether or not anyone is wearing it. And it can be operated by persons not wearing the garment.

I would suggest that *Remote Control I* challenges us to think about the meaning(s) of clothing in a way that is relevant to the study of contemporary quilted garments. Interpreting the meaning(s) of any quilted garment involves careful consideration of 1) what the garment might communicate on the body of the artist in particular contexts and what she aims to communicate with the garment; 2) what the garment communicates independent of the artist's body or her intentions; and 3) how people other than the artist shape its meaning(s).

Looking at the outfits some contemporary quilt artists are creating in light of the titles they are assigning their work, I see an emergent materialist feminist voice creating a space for real age-, class-, and race-specific women to experience their "bodies" and their "selves" outside conventional, dominant cultural narratives. But I am concerned that the way these garments are represented in style shows sometimes mutes the voice that I want and need to hear.

Acknowledgments

Thanks to Laurel Horton and Virginia Gunn for their editorial comments and to Virginia Avery, Elinor Peace Bailey, Debbie Driscoll, and Donna Wilder for their contributions to this essay.

Notes and References

1. Jill Dolan, *The Feminist Spectator As Critic*, (Ann Arbor: UMI Research, 1988).
2. Lorre Marie Weidlich, "Quilting Transformed: An Anthropological Approach to the Quilt Revival" (Ph.D. thesis, University of Texas–Austin, 1986), 69-77.
3. At the Houston quilt festival, for example, embellished garments are formally presented at the invitational Fairfield/Concord Fashion Show, in a non-juried fashion show in which garmentmakers model their own creations, and at show and tell sessions. All information about the Fairfield/Concord Fashion Show was obtained in phone interviews with Debbie Driscoll (September 7, 1989) and Donna Wilder (February 14, 1990).
4. The annual invitational fashion show at the Houston Quilt Festival is jointly sponsored by Fairfield Processing Corporation–manufacturer of batting–and Concord Fabrics. The subsequent tour of the show is made possible by Fairfield Processing Corporation alone.
5. For discussions of clothing as politically resistant, see Grant McCracken, *Culture and Consumption: New Approaches to the Symbolic Character of Consumer Goods and Activities* (Bloomington: Indiana University Press, 1988); and Kaja Silverman, "Fragments of a Fashionable Discourse" in *Studies in Entertainment: Critical Approaches to Mass Culture*, ed. Tania Modleski (Bloomington: Indiana University Press, 1986).

6. It should be noted that, while the title of Masopust's garment seems to constitute the coat as a kind of critique of the way in which Henry VIII's wives were done away with, the coat **must** be accompanied by the title to have this meaning. Henry VIII is displayed most prominently on the center/back of the coat, while his wives are relegated to the coat's edges. Masopust saves the queens, but in the same position they always were, relative to Henry VIII.
7. Laura Mulvey, "Visual Pleasure and Narrative Cinema" *Screen* 16 (1975), 3:6-18.
8. Teresa de Lauretis, *Alice Doesn't: Feminism, Semiotics, Cinema*, (Bloomington: Indiana University Press, 1984); and E. Ann Kaplan, "Is the Gaze Male?" in *Powers of Desire: The Politics of Sexuality*, ed. Snitow, Stansell & Thompson, (New York: Monthly Review Press, 1983), 309-27.
9. This is not to suggest that all events at quilt conferences need be introduced by women. I find the idea of more men quilting, more men at quilt festivals, and more men giving introductions to quilt events perfectly acceptable, even desirable. Had Michael James introduced the show, I don't think I'd have flinched. But, to me, Gleitman represented "the male gaze" in the form of a corporate seal of approval.
10. These sexually suggestive messages were not unambiguous. With *Midsummer Night's Dream*, the quilted and embellished panel that hung in front from the waist to the floor functioned in counterpoint to the low neckline, seeming to guard and block access to that part of the female body. Similarly, the multilayered, heavily embellished petals of the skirt of *Pavo Cristatus* made it appear impenetrable.
11. The commentary usually provided by Donna Wilder at the Houston festival apparently focuses much more on the techniques of garment construction and embellishment used by the quilt artist.
12. That women of color were not "models" or otherwise visible at Quilt Expo Europa is, of course, no one's fault. It is simply an observation I believe worth considering. In fact, the Fairfield/Concord show stage in Houston has, for the past several years, featured an African-American model.
13. The slides for the 1988 fashion show were taken by Brad Stanton. The fact that he is a man, however, is not what constructs the male gaze. It is the fact that the women in the slides are posed in a way that suggests they are doing nothing but showing their bodies, their "selves" for men.
14. Virginia Avery, interview with author, New York, NY, October 4, 1989.
15. Donna Wilder believes that the vast majority of women who design

and make garments for the Fairfield/Concord Fashion Show do not do so with their own bodies in mind.
16. Kate Davy, "Buying and Selling the LOOK," *PARACHUTE* (Summer 1986):22–24. See also Frigga Haug's *Female Sexualization*, trans. Erica Carter (London: Verso Books, 1983).
17. Virginia Avery, "Hot Time in Houston: Inside a Fairfield Fashion Show Extravaganza." *Threads Magazine* 25 (October/November 1989): 50–51.
18. For a description of prairie points, see *Quiter's Newsletter Magazine*, no. 154, 30.
19. Elizabeth Ewen and Stuart Ewen, *Channels of Desire: Mass Images and the Shaping of American Consciousness*, (New York: McGraw-Hill, 1982).
20. Eleanor Peace Bailey, telephone interview, October 7, 1989.
21. Wilder indicates that, in fact, many garments made for the show are not a size ten, but more a size twelve. This might indicate that many women are being "creative" about finding solutions to the problems this rule potentially poses.
22. I found it ironic and disturbing that not one artist referred to in the categories was a woman.
23. Donna Wilder indicates that her aim, when selecting music, is to find upbeat instrumental pieces that the audience will recognize.

The Julia Boyer Reinstein Collection

Nancilu B. Burdick

In 1987 Julia Boyer Reinstein, historian and architectural preservationist of Cheektowaga, New York, gave seventy-four quilts and eighteen other bed coverings to the Buffalo and Erie County Historical Society. The donation represents the major part of a quilt collection acquired over a sixty-year period. The collection is unusual in that only twelve of the quilts were purchased, the rest having come to Julia through gifts or inheritance. In addition to the purchased quilts, Julia donated twenty-six inherited family quilts and thirty-six quilts that had been gifts to herself or to her mother, Julia Smith Mason. Except for two family quilts made in other states, the Reinstein Collection consists entirely of Western New York quilts, most of them made in the Genesee River Valley area where Julia grew up and where her maternal ancestors had lived for five generations. Sixty-six of the quilts are pieced, and only two are appliqued. The collection also includes two whole-cloth and four embroidered quilts.

Julia's marked preference for pieced quilts correlates with her interest in architecture. Pieced quilts are designed and assembled in units to fit the aesthetic perceptions of the maker, much as a well designed building is conceived by its architect before construction. "The mathematical precision, improvisational skills, and creative ingenuity represented by the complexity of the pieced quilt are qualities which make them unique among the folk arts," Julia said, explaining the make-up of her collection. "Particular recognition is due those nineteenth and early twentieth century quiltmakers because much of their work was a salvage craft."[1] Mary Arnold Twining, who curated an exhibit of some of Julia's quilts in 1986, agrees. "Since often their material was limited by what was available locally and within

---

Nancilu B. Burdick, 35 Countryside Lane #8, Orchard Park NY 14127.

the family, often bits and pieces left over from other projects, scraps of worn out garments and bedding, there is a documentary function which they serve in intimate family history."[2]

Julia Reinstein is quick to give credit to her maternal forebears, beginning with her great-great-grandmother, Elizabeth Havens Pickett, for the continuing tradition of quiltmaking which culminated in Julia's stewardship five generations later of thirty-five family quilts. Her earliest memory is of her maternal grandmother, Agnes Pickett Smith "threading hundreds of needles for me as I sat on a stool beside her to piece and embroider some crazy quilt blocks. I was only three or four years old. From that time on I have always been aware of quilts."[3] Julia's long involvement with preserving Western New York quilts fits well into the life for which her nature, education, and family background prepared her.

Julia's maternal ancestors, the Picketts, came to Wyoming County, New York, in the fall of 1817, just twenty years after the Council of Big Tree in which the Seneca Indians gave up their tribal lands.[4] James Pickett and his brother Daniel, veterans of the Revolutionary War and the War of 1812, were on their way to Michigan from Washington County, New York. Because James Pickett's wife Elizabeth was expecting a child during the winter, the party made camp in the settlement of Castile, and the men found employment with a sawmill.

By spring 1818 James Pickett was so impressed with the area he had decided to remain in the scenic Genesee River Valley, while his brother continued the journey and settled in Munith, Michigan. During the winter Elizabeth Havens Pickett had given birth to a boy, Daniel, Julia Reinstein's great-grandfather, and had completed a quilt begun back in Washington County.[5] The pink and white quilt, called Rob Peter to Pay Paul, Hearts Version (family name), was destined to come down through generations of Picketts to Julia and to be the spark that ignited her burning interest in quilts and the women who made them. It is the oldest quilt in the Reinstein Collection, and family folklore says it was completed while camping in the Genesee Valley.

By 1919 when Julia was twelve years old, the treasured quilt was beginning to show the ravages of time and use. Julia's mother, a busy schoolteacher and occasional quilter, decided then to make an "exact copy" of the old quilt for her only daughter. Looking about for suitable material, Julia Smith Mason bought the last of a bolt of pink cotton fabric in a country store in Gainesville, New York, just a few miles from her home in Silver Springs. When she unwrapped the cloth she was astonished to find a bill of sale dating the fabric to 1866. Impatient to have the quilt completed, Julia Mason paid Mrs. Lydia Hall, also of Silver Springs, to make the quilt.[6]

Julia Reinstein was born in Buffalo, New York, on March 3, 1907, and grew up in Wyoming County, the fifth generation of a family of strong and independent women.

Her grandmother's sister, Julia Pickett Norris and her husband, Fred Norris, "practically raised" Julia from the age of nineteen months. Her Uncle Fred made her vividly aware of the Genesee Valley area's impressive natural beauty and pioneer heritage, and doubtless influenced Julia's interests and tastes more than any other person in her life.

In 1928 Julia received her BA degree in History from Elmira College for Women and wrote her senior thesis on early American quilts. At the time Julia did not know that Ruth E. Finley was about to complete her landmark book on patchwork quilts.[7] But she was well aware of the prominent Mrs. Jessie Farrall Peck of Bergen, Genesee County, an authority on quilts and other antiques and an avid collector. Peck had bought the historic Jane D. Waldron Castile quilt in 1920 for $10.00.[8]

"The Castile quilt was a key part of my paper. I had heard of the fabulous Peck collection, and Mrs. Peck allowed me to study that quilt and the history of its maker." Julia was to become the owner of that quilt and nine other Peck quilts after Mrs. Peck's death in 1954.

In 1939, after a decade of teaching and travel, Julia came to teach history in the Buffalo suburb of Cheektowaga, New York. Julia was to devote herself increasingly through public service to the people of that township for half a century.

Two significant mileposts in Julia's life occurred in 1942. At age thirty-five she received her Master of Arts degree in History from Columbia University, and she married Dr. Victor Reinstein, a prominent physician and naturalist in Cheektowaga. Dr. Reinstein, the son of Ukrainian immigrants, took his bride to an old, rambling fourteen-room house on the edge of his 280-acre nature preserve, where he lived with his mother, Dr. Anna Reinstein, an obstetrician, and a young son by his first wife. Julia brought with her a number of family quilts she had already inherited or that had been made for her. She would later need more room than even that big house afforded for her growing collection.

Some years later, while teaching history at the University of Buffalo, Julia began work on a PhD degree, "but my daughter came along in 1948 and ended that pursuit." Julia Reinstein named her daughter Julia Anna "for Aunt Julia who raised me, and to carry on the name of my great-grandmother's favorite cousin in Syracuse whom everyone loved."

While at Columbia Julia had written a research paper on early American textiles used in quilts. She made trips to Bergen, near Rochester, to study Mrs. Peck's quilt collection, and to Wyoming County to study her own family's quilts. She also spent time at the Metropolitan Museum of Art to study a rare old Star of Bethlehem. "The Metropolitan considered such a quilt, if well pieced and nicely quilted, the epitome of perfection." Because of this and other research over the years Julia became known as an expert on early American quilts. In the early 1950s she was invited to be a consultant at the Seminars on American History at Cooperstown, New York. It was in that informal setting that she met Ruth E. Finley and "spent a great deal of time with her, taking some of my quilts for her to identify." The two women became friends and correspondents, often talking quilts by phone, until Finley's death in 1955. Julia, not knowing how famous Ruth Finley would become, does not remember saving her letters.

Quilts that were gifts to Julia or to her mother make up the major part of the Reinstein Collection. In 1960 Julia was given a Star of Bethlehem as a gift from her best friend, Gladys Boag Butler. The quilt was made in 1871 by Butler's great-aunt, Jane Patterson Boag of Steuben County. That quilt was one of numerous quilts Julia acquired over the years by gifts that seemed to fall like blessings into her life, once people learned that she cared deeply about quilts as historical documents and would preserve them. "Beginning in the early 1960s, I must have given twenty-five or thirty lectures on my quilts, and often people would come up and tell me about their old family quilts. Some would give them to me because they knew I would treasure them, no matter what age or condition. At that time I decided not to take any that were not made in New York State. I wanted to know the maker and provenance, and began to limit my collection to Western New York quilts."

The publicity accorded Julia locally as a woman intensely interested in quilts brought her such a large and varied assortment that the quilts began to overrun the house. To contain them, Victor Reinstein built large pine chests in the upper story of a stone lodge in the Reinstein woods. In that unheated stone house the quilts continued to accumulate and remained for more than twenty years.

One quilt added to Julia's collection in the early 1960s was a well-preserved Tumbling Blocks signed O. J. and dated 1900, that had been given to Dr. Anna Reinstein by one of her patients. Another was presented to Julia, after she had given a talk, by the granddaughter of Mr. Stapley who was from a family of Livingston County tenant farmers. Stapley made the unusual cotton Crazy Quilt in 1910–1911 and embroidered it quite simply along the seams, backing it, without filler, with a printed cotton fabric. A wonderful Caesar's Crown made in red, white, green, and gold by Maria Weitz of Cheektowaga in the 1870s or earlier was presented to Julia by the maker's great-granddaughter. Weitz and her husband Wilhelm had migrated from Germany in 1871, and the quilt may have been made or at least begun in Germany.[9]

By the mid-1960s Julia's collection had grown to more than seventy quilts, and groups for whom she gave talks were amazed to see a tall, strong, vibrant woman bring in bag after bag of quilts retrieved from the stone lodge, joyously using them to illustrate her lectures.

"One very stormy February afternoon after a newspaper article about my collection, Mrs. Daniel Baker of Shoshone Avenue, Buffalo, phoned me. She brought me a package of fifty Pan-American Penny Blocks, embroidered in 1901–1902 by Mrs. Baker's sister Arlene Kay at age seven." The stamped blocks were sold during the Pan-American Exposition in Buffalo in 1901. Julia had forty-eight of the best blocks assembled into twin quilts by Mrs. Chris Lenz of Cheektowaga.

Julia's friend, Gladys Boag Butler, having no descendants, decided about 1965 to give Julia two more of her grandmother's quilts. A Blind Man's Fancy, its blocks intricately pieced with many variations, and assembled with Flying Geese sashing and four borders,

Figure 1. *Pan American Penny Block*. Embroidered in 1901–1902 by Arlene Kay, age seven, from stamped penny block squares sold at the 1901 Pan-American Exposition in Buffalo, NY. Sold in complete sets of 50 blocks, these were a gift to Julia Reinstein in the mid-1960s.

was made in the 1880s by Mrs. Marie Boag of Canisteo, Steuben County. Julia describes it as "a complex picture of perfection." An Old Maid's Puzzle, given to Gladys's mother by a Mrs. Schule of Angelica was made in the late 1860s and given to Marie Boag "about the time Gladys was born."

Some years before Julia's mother died in 1955, she gave her daughter two more quilts that had been gifts to her. A Sunburst variation was pieced in 1900–1910 by someone in the Wells family of Pike, New York, but was never quilted. "It came from the family of Elbert Hubbard's second wife, and Ruth Finley gave it the name of Lone Star Gone Crazy. I was at a loss to identify the pattern, so I sent it to Ruth Finley with a letter asking her help; Ruth returned it with a reply, the last letter I received from her. I wrote her once more and my letter was returned marked 'deceased.'" A Rob Peter to Pay Paul, Hexagon Version in deep red and white made in 1910 by Elizabeth Partridge of Genesee Falls had been given to Julia Mason shortly before her death.

The "Family Quilts" in the BECHS Reinstein collection include both much used "work quilts" and also special quilts that came down to Julia in prime condition. A Chimney Sweep, intended to be a friendship album quilt commemorating her popular young womanhood in Castile, was pieced in 1850–1854 by Julia's maternal great-grandmother Eliza Jane Graves. The blocks were originally autographed by young men of the community at quilting parties, a customary Genesee Valley practice in the mid-nineteenth century. Before Eliza Jane had embroidered the names, she was betrothed to Daniel Pickett, who did not fancy sleeping under other men's signatures, some of them his former rivals. So after her marriage in 1854, Eliza Jane carefully washed out all the names and assembled the quilt, finishing it with her own handspun, hand-loomed backing. Afterward, it was considered a "work quilt" which Julia herself slept under as a child.

Eliza Jane's sister-in-law, Martha Jane Armstrong Pickett, of Munith, Michigan, made a Double Jacob's Ladder (usually called Double Irish Chain) in red and white, and put the final stitches in it on April 14, 1865, the day President Lincoln was shot. Always called "the Lincoln quilt," it is a repertory of Martha Jane's quilting skills, each white block displaying a different design. Julia Reinstein was astonished to receive this "historic" quilt in 1928 in the mail from

Figure 2. *Chimney Sweep*. Made in 1852–1853 by Eliza Jane Graves in Perry, Wyoming County, NY. Originally signed in pencil by male friends, their names were washed out after Eliza Jane's marriage to Daniel Pickett, Julia Reinstein's great-grandfather.

Martha Jane's unmarried daughter, after Aunt Julia had persuaded her niece to give a talk on some of the family quilts at a Pickett family reunion in Michigan. That was Julia's first "quilt talk," and she was only twenty-one. "I didn't want to do it but Aunt Julia insisted. So we drove in style with the car full of quilts. Aunt Julia was an iron fist in a velvet glove and she had her way."

In the 1860s, Anna Marie Strauss Strickrott, Julia's paternal great-grandmother, pieced a "complex version of the Rob-Peter-to-Pay-Paul" pattern, the name family tradition has always associated with the quilt. Anna Marie used blue fabrics her husband John Christopher Strickrott had designed for a German textile mill before the family's migration to the United States in 1861, and he may also have designed the quilt pattern. The quilt was one of sixteen quilt tops made

Figure 3. *Rob-Peter-to-Pay-Paul, Complex Variation* (family name). Pieced in 1860–1864 by Marie Strauss Strickrott in Connecticut, quilted in 1924 by Anna Margaret Strickrott in Missouri. Some of the fabrics and, perhaps, the pattern itself are said to have been designed by Christopher Strickrott, the maker's husband.

for the youngest daughter's dowry chest. It was a Strickrott family custom for mothers to piece one quilt top a year for each daughter until her seventeenth birthday. It was the daughter's responsibility to quilt them. Anna Margaret, Julia's grandmother, was just three years old in 1861 and within a few years the family moved to Ohio, where Anna Margaret grew up, married Richard McNight Boyer, and moved with him to Missouri. She and her husband prospered, and Anna Margaret was in her sixties before, as Julia described, "she decided in the 1920s to quilt all her dowry tops for her own granddaughters. There were six of us so there are fifteen more of her quilts who knows where."

Over the years, Anna Margaret Boyer and her mother had accumulated many odd blocks not used for the dowry and other family quilts, some machine-pieced by Anna Margaret, some made by hand "way back in Germany" by Anna Marie Strauss. When Julia Reinstein visited her grandmother in Trenton, Missouri in 1932, Anna

Margaret was seventy-four, "and she was at last putting those blocks together as a Sampler quilt—just to save them." The colorful quilt contains thirty-six odd-sized blocks, five of which are pieced in variations of the ancient swastika symbol. "I begged her to let me have the top, just as it was for I never wanted it quilted," Julia said. "I attached a heavy sleeve to the quilt—and it was the one family quilt my daughter wanted for a wall hanging."

Julia inherited a number of quilts made especially for her aunt, Julia Pickett Norris, who died in 1956. Hannah Graves, Julia Reinstein's great-grandmother's unmarried sister, made quilts for all her nieces and nephews. She made both a Variable Star and a Wine Glass for niece Julia Pickett. The Variable Star scrap quilt was made in the mid-1860s when "Aunt Julia" was just an infant. Hannah Graves filled it with hand-carded wool from the Daniel Pickett Farm near Perry, where she spent the last years of her life. She completed the red and white Wine Glass in October 1881, and filled it with thin cotton batting, for it was intended as a summer quilt. According to Julia "the arrangement of the baskets toward the center indicates it was made for a 'work quilt' which could be turned end to end for longer wear, and always look the same."

In all, Julia inherited six quilts made by her great-grandmother, Eliza Jane Graves Pickett. A Four Patch she made between 1895 and 1900 when she was an old woman, is typical of numerous turn-of-the-century quilts made in the Genesee Valley. It is a "common scrap quilt" intended to be used and worn out, and Julia remembers it as one of her favorite quilts to sleep under as a child, perhaps because of the equestrian and tennis prints in the sashing and in some blocks. The backing is pieced in alternating blue striped and brown checked strips, 12-to-14-inches wide, left over from other projects. The quilting is fine and even, and the quilt is very well preserved.

Of the "Smith family quilts" Julia inherited, one is a Chinese Coin made in Castile, 1875–1876, by her maternal grandmother, Agnes Pickett Smith, shortly before Frederick Smith II moved with his family to Nebraska. In fine condition, the multi-colored scrap quilt, inherited first by Julia Mason and then by Julia herself, is quilted "in-the-ditch" with a cotton blanket filling and a one-piece muslin backing.

Julia Smith Boyer's marriage to Charles R. Mason of Silver Springs in 1914, made her heir to his family's quilts, most of them "Methodist Church quilts" not considered worth preserving. The predominantly pink and dark blue Wagon Tracks (a variation of Jacob's Ladder) was one of four quilts found resting between mattresses and springs of double beds. Yet the Wagon Tracks, made in the first quarter of the twentieth century, was thought worthy of conservation by the Buffalo and Erie Historical Society.

Several privately-owned family quilts document intimate family history. The precisely structured Grade Crossing, usually called Hovering Hawks, which contains a scrapbag of materials left over from family aprons, shirts, and housedresses, has an interesting personal history. The quilt was instrumental in Julia's recovery from a long and severe case of influenza during World War I. To keep her quietly occupied she was allowed to pick out scraps that held memories for her, scraps saved over many years from sewing family clothing. Much of the original cloth came from Julia's step-father's store in Castile. Mother and daughter then chose the pattern and Julia Mason and Mrs. Lydia Hall, a neighbor, make the quilt for Julia for Christmas. It was also her "recovery present." Women have recognized this healing function of handmade quilts throughout their long unrecorded history.[10]

Julia herself, who learned to sew from her grandmother, made several quilts, one of which she intended as an heirloom. She made the brilliant red-and-white Railroad Crossing in 1948–1950, from fine Egyptian cotton purchased for her in London by a friend. She made it for her daughter Julia Anna's birth present, and had it quilted by ladies of the Hamburg Methodist Church.

Julia Pickett Norris pieced many quilts while her niece Julia was growing up. Four of Aunt Julia's tops were never quilted. They were "lost" when Fred and Julia Norris moved from Castile to Warsaw in 1911. "Aunt Julia worried and worried over those lost tops, and after her death in 1956, and my uncle's a year earlier, I rented out the Norris house in Warsaw." Julia decided to sell the house in 1961. Still concerned about the "lost quilts," she and her thirteen-year old daughter Julia Anna, turned the house inside out to no avail. Just as Julia was about to hand over the keys to the new owners, she remembered a remote crawl space in one unlighted corner of the attic. Young Julia Anna wedged her way through and "there, lo and behold, was a wooden shirtwaist box with Aunt Julia's quilt tops and one finished quilt right where they had been summer and winter for fifty years, undamaged after all that time." The one finished quilt found in the attic is thought to be one of the last quilts made by Eliza Jane Graves Pickett, Julia's great-grandmother.

In addition to quilts acquired as gifts and inherited through the family, the twelve purchased quilts are an important part of the Reinstein Collection. Ten of those came from the Jessie Farrall Peck Auction in Bergen, New York. After Mrs. Peck's death in 1954, a widely publicized auction was held of her huge and important antiques collection.

Julia's purchases reflect her interest in women's history and in originality and precision of workmanship. Seven are pieced, two are appliqued, and one is whole cloth. Both applique quilts are interesting variations of the Charter Oak design. In the late 1840s Sarah Haight of Mechanicsville, New York, made one in red and white from a hand-cut original pattern. It displays exquisite quilting, eleven stitches per inch. The second, a traditional Oak Leaf and Reel in green and white was hand-made in 1835–1837 by a relative of Mrs. Peck in Bergen. The block design was cut from tin patterns which were sold separately at the auction. The handsome bird-and-tree borders were made from original patterns hand-cut by the maker.[11] The quilting of leaf and flower shapes echoes the leaf design in the green fabric.

The Castile quilt made by Jane D. Waldron in 1848 is one of two Castile quilts, their designs created entirely of large pieced letters patterned after the cross-stitched lettering found in old samplers.[12] Jane D. Waldron was brought from England to the United States at the age of five. She was "bound out" at age twelve to Judge Rose of Castile and soon became one of the family. She completed her quilt at age twenty in 1848. Four years later she married Mr. J. Truesdale and went with him to Michigan. Jane Waldron Truesdale died in Michigan in childbirth, along with her only child, and the quilt was returned to the Truesdale family in Warsaw, from whom Mrs. Peck bought it.

The single whole-cloth quilt purchased from the Peck Collection reflects an era of self-sufficiency. The blue quilt was made in 1845 by a Peck relative, completely by hand from "handspun, home-woven, and home-dyed cotton materials, and filled with home-carded and dyed wool from the farm sheep." Its interesting local history and fine workmanship appealed to Julia even though the quilt was faded.

Two other Peck quilts illustrate Julia's interest in pieced precision, aesthetic judgments, and the fine workmanship of women during those times when intelligent thought was not preceived as their domain. A Delectable Mountains was made by Hepzibah Prentice in 1848–1850, in Alexander, Genesee County, New York. The quilt is expertly assembled with green vertical sashing. With corners cut out for a four-poster bed, the quilt is framed on three sides by a striking Cactus Rose border, making it an artistically and technically fine creation. A Pineapple variation made between 1864 and 1865 by a Mrs. VanDerhagen, Middlebury, Wyoming County, is filled with thick, hand-carded cotton, and exhibits superb piecing and quilting skills. Except for the unstable green and red that have faded to a warm beige and dusty rose, the quilt is in excellent condition.

In 1987, when Julia Boyer Reinstein decided on the Buffalo and Erie County Historical Society as a repository for her quilts and bed coverings, she was already deeply involved in another passionate interest: photographic documentation and preservation of New York State's historic architecture. As a member of the Historical Society's Board of Managers she received its prestigious Red Jacket Award in 1974. That award is presented annually to recognize "a lifetime of quiet, continued unbroken devotion" to civic progress.[13]

Those words are an apt description of this dynamic, eighty-three year old woman. Although beset by a number of serious health problems, she continues to pursue an active life, giving generously of her time, energy, and resources to public service. She has been a coveted speaker and panelist for many professional conferences, including the 1987 and 1988 annual meetings of the American Association of State and Local History. The New York State Historical Association honored her in November 1988 with the first Albert Corey Award for distinguished service by a local historian. She has been the moving force behind the Erie County Historical Federation since she founded it in 1950 and has been involved personally in establishing twenty-five town historical societies throughout the county.

Julia has a strong interest in conservation as well as historic preservation. After her husband's death in 1984 she held in trust for the

Figure 4. Julia Reinstein with *Delectable Mountains* quilt, made by Hepzibah Prentice in 1848–1850. From the Jessie Farrall Peck Collection. (Photograph by Thomas Payne, used with permission of Buffalo and Erie County Historical Society.)

State of New York a large tract of land she and Dr. Reinstein had preserved in its natural wooded state as a part of their Cheektowaga property.[14] She is so involved in preserving Erie County's historical and natural heritage, she has been called the "community's historical conscience."[15] During 1989 she was actively assisting in the preparation of a book on Erie County architecture, and helping to plan an exhibit of the Buffalo Historical Society's quilts for 1990.

The gift of Julia Reinstein's quilts has contributed significantly to the Buffalo Historical Society's quilt collection, more than doubling its numbers and greatly increasing its representation of Western New

York quilts. Largely without words, the quilts record for our own and future generations the ingenuity, resourcefulness, and perseverance of women of Western New York. They also reflect Julia Reinstein's strong interest in history, her own tastes and personality, as well as her family background. Some are also historically important as strong links to the past of this region.

Notes and References

1. Julia Boyer Reinstein, interview by author, tape recording, Buffalo and Erie County Historical Society, September 21, 1988.
2. Mary Arnold Twining, "Introduction," *Checkered Paths* exhibition booklet, Buffalo State College, September, 1986.
3. Reinstein interview.
4. Henry W. Clune, *The Genesee* (New York: Holt, Rinehart and Winston, 1963), 110–126.
5. Julia Reinstein, interview by author, tape recording, Cheektowaga, New York, November 16, 1988. (Subsequent quotations throughout this paper unless otherwise credited, are from above interviews, or from a third interview on May 19, 1989.)
6. The 1919 Rob Peter to Pay Paul, Hearts Version was one of nine quilts retained by Julia Reinstein.
7. Ruth E. Finley, *Old Patchwork Quilts and the Women Who Made Them*, Reprint, (Newton Centre, MA: Charles T. Branford, 1929, reprint 1983).
8. Jessie Farrall Peck wrote articles on her collection for *Good Housekeeping*, *House Beautiful*, and *Antiques* in the 1930s. Richard Peck, Monroe, TN. Telephone interview by author December 29, 1989.
9. Patsy Orlofsky, of The Textile Conservation Workshop, dates this quilt to the mid-nineteenth century. See also Carter Houck and Myron Miller, *American Quilts* (New York: Charles Scribner's Sons, 1975), 108, for a similar 1870s quilt, said to be of German origin.
10. Nancilu B. Burdick, *Legacy, The Story of Talula Gilbert Bottoms and Her Quilts*, (Nashville: Rutledge Hill, 1988), 143, 144–146.
11. Mrs. Peck's notes on her collection were given to Julia Reinstein by Mrs. Peck's son some years after her death.
12. See also Patsy and Myron Orlofsky, *Quilts in America*, (New York: McGraw Hill, 1974), 216, 283; Carleton Safford and Robert Bishop, *America's Quilts and Coverlets* (New York: E. P. Dutton, 1980), 137; and Winifred Reddall, "Pieced Lettering on Seven Quilts Dating from 1833

to 1891" in *Uncoverings* 1980, ed. Sally Garoutte, (Mill Valley, CA: American Quilt Study Group, 1981), 56-63.
13. Red Jacket Award Recipient Named, *Newsletter*, ed. Cherie Messore, (Buffalo and Erie County Historical Society, Fall 1974), 3.
14. The Reinstein Woods, a 280 acre nature preserve was officially turned over to the State of New York on August 23, 1989.
15. Dr. William Seiner, quoted in "Julia Reinstein Receives Statewide Recognition", *Newsletter*, ed. Cherie Messore, (Buffalo and Erie County Historical Society, Fall 1988), 6.

Appendix

The Five Generations of Quiltmakers in Julia Reinstein's Family (M = Maternal; P = Paternal)

		NAME	SPOUSE
I.		Elizabeth Havens Pickett (b 1786) great-great-grandmother (M)	James Pickett
II.	1.	Eliza Jane Graves Pickett (1833-1910) great-grandmother (M)	Daniel Pickett
	2.	Elizabeth Strong Pickett great-great-aunt (Eliza Jane's sister-in-law)	
	3.	Rebecca Mills Smith (great-grandmother) (M)	Frederick Smith I
	4.	Anna Marie Strauss Strickrott (b. 1817 in Germany) great-grandmother (P)	Christopher Strickrott
	5.	Martha Jane Armstrong Pickett great-great-aunt (M)	Albert Pickett
	6.	Hannah Graves great-great-aunt (M)	Unmarried
III.	1.	Agnes Pickett Smith grandmother (1860-1914) (M)	Frederick Smith II
	2.	Anna Margaret Strickrott Boyer grandmother (b. 1858) (P)	Richard McKnight Boyer
	3.	Julia Anna Pickett Norris great aunt (1865?-1956) (M)	Fred Norris
IV.		Julia Smith (Boyer) Mason mother (1886-1955)	Lee Boyer, Charles Mason
V.		Julia Boyer Reinstein (1907-)	Dr. Victor Reinstein

Mourning Quilts in America

Gail Andrews Trechsel

Quilts have been the constant companions of American women for over two centuries, created for all occasions, giving comfort day to day. Women made quilts to commemorate births and marriages, to honor community leaders and friends, and to memorialize the dead. Quilts in this last group, mourning quilts, provided the maker with a tangible memorial to the departed and sometimes served a practical purpose in the burial process or the home.

Death's toll in both eighteenth- and nineteenth-century America was formidable. However, acceptance and accomodation to death varied greatly from one century to another. In the American colonies in the eighteenth century, mourning rituals tended to be simple. The family prepared the deceased for burial in the home, and both men and women were expected to have a matter-of-fact attitude towards death. Verses wrought into samplers by young girls often alluded to the makers' mortality. Children's toys sometimes took a form we would consider morbid today: toy coffins, often with removable figures, were acceptable playthings.[1]

The advent of the Romantic movement at the end of the eighteenth century resulted in a different way of viewing death and memorializing those it took away. Death was romanticized, mourning became more elaborate and new memorials were created for the deceased.[2] Mourning pictures in needlework and watercolor became popular and were made in great numbers by young women with sufficient time and leisure. These pictures were based upon classic Greek models and included standard motifs, such as urns set on inscribed tombstones in a landscape with weeping willows, and mourning figures, usually female, bowed in grief, near the tombstone.

Gail Andrews Trechsel, 3406 Altamont Way, Birmingham AL 35205.

In addition, the Romantic movement stressed the expression of feelings, and young women created sentimental representations which echoed the views expressed in popular literature of the day.

As people began to sentimentalize death, they also began to domesticate heaven, which became known as a "home beyond the skies," a domestic world particularly suited to Victorian women.[3] Heaven was no longer a place to fear one's judgment; it became another home, offering a place for a reunion with the dear departed. Novels even offered homey descriptions of heaven complete with household essentials.

Compatible with this sentimental and domestic view of heaven was the ideology, prevalent by the 1830s, of the Cult of True Womanhood, or the Cult of Domesticity. As individuals romanticized death, they also defined separate spheres for men and women. No longer was woman simply man's helpmeet as she had been in the eighteenth century. She was instead removed from the world of trade and commerce and encouraged to pursue "indoor pursuits (which) would harmonize with her natural love of home and its duties."[4] Her role was to care for the home and rear the children; she was the preserver of home and hearth.

Women were viewed as more pious, sensitive, and generally closer to heaven than men. As such, women became the primary mourners. A woman writing at the end of the nineteenth century complained that a wife often stayed home in mourning while her husband went to a party, even though it was his blood relation who had died. And further, "the custom of mourning presses far more heavily on women than men. In fact, so trifling are the alterations made in a man's dress . . . that practically the whole burden of mourning wrappings would seem to have fallen on women. . . . They (men) positively manage to mourn by proxy!"[5]

The rituals of burial and mourning became more elaborate in the early nineteenth century. Tombstones sometimes bore portraits of the deceased; and angels, willow tress, urns, garlands, and weeping survivors became appropriate ornaments. Nineteenth century imagery contrasts sharply with the stark symbols of earlier gravestones: skulls, death masks, and empty hourglasses. It also became proper to preserve reminders of the deceased in the home. Mourning pictures and posthumous portraits and photographs were frequently

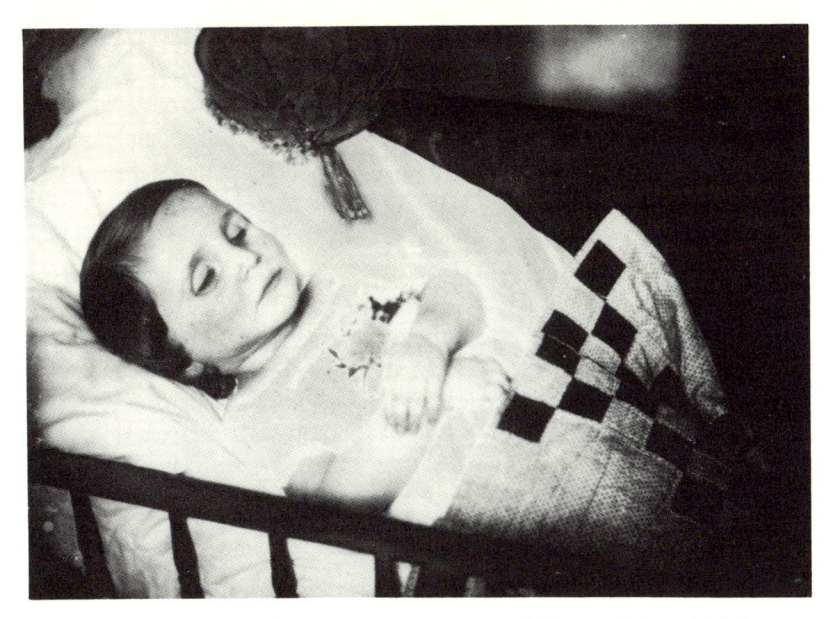

Figure. 1. Posthumous daguerreotype portrait of George Henry Williams, son of Henry C. and Diana T. Williams, who died at age 18 months. Collection of the State Historical Society of Wisconsin, gift of Irving Brown.

executed for the grieving family. These pictures became a way of holding onto lives too soon ended. Portraits of children were especially popular.

The posthumous photograph, often displayed in the home, could be placed on a mantel or table in the sitting room. Grace Snyder, describing her life in frontier Nebraska, recalls walking into the home of her future husband's family: "Big family photographs in heavy frames hung on the living room walls. Among them was one of the little dead William, and another of a sister who had died on the West Coast."[6]

Mourning customs and costume of the nineteenth century were carefully developed by the time Queen Victoria ascended the British throne in 1837. However, no one mourned with greater intensity or dedication than she. In 1861, the Queen lost both her mother and her husband. After Prince Albert's death Victoria wore mourning dress for the remaining forty years of her life. Every bed in which Victoria slept had, at the back, on the right-hand side, above the pillow, a photograph of the head and shoulders of Prince Albert as he lay dead, crowned by a wreath of dried flowers.[7] The Queen commissioned a succession of monuments and memorials to Albert, but it is perhaps the private shrine Victoria created for him that tells us most about her grief and her obesion:

> The suite of rooms which Albert had occupied in the Castle was kept for ever shut away from the eyes of any save the most privileged. Within those precincts everything remained as it had been at the Prince's death; but the mysterious preoccupation of Victoria had commanded that her husband's clothing should be laid afresh, each evening, the water should be set ready in the basin, as if he were still alive; and this incredible rite was performed with scrupulous regularity for nearly forty years.[8]

Queen Victoria fostered the cult of mourning, spreading it among all classes during her lifetime. Published accounts of the Queen's faithfulness had a tremendous effect on people, and her example was followed by many of her subjects.[9] While other women did not have this kind of power, position, or wealth to devote to their grief, outward manifestations of sorrow were customary and expected. Mourning customs controlled one's dress, social life, and the interior of one's home. Quilts in black and white and shades of gray, usually with a black border, were often made to replace the brightly-colored calicoes. Some individuals even used black sheets for their beds during deep mourning.[10] It is probable that these quilts were passed among families as need arose. Mourning quilts appear to have been more common in America during the second half of nineteenth century than earlier.

Quilt historian Dr. William R. Dunton, Jr., discovered four mourning quilts made by Mrs. Julia Ann Cromer Flickinger (1827-1901). Mrs. Flickinger lived near New Windsor, Maryland, and was a prodigious quilter and seamstress. At her death she left 150 quilts, 100 of which were finished, so that her four children received 25 quilts each as part of their inheritance.

Dr. Dunton states that Mrs. Flickinger made four quilts in black and white which she used during mourning following the death of her husband in 1896. Dr. Dunton describes one of Mrs Flickinger's quilts, called Midnight Star:

> The quilt measures six feet ten inches by seven feet and is bound with the lining material. The five-inch border is of a black and white striped calico, and the alternate blocks are of black with a fine white line in which occur tiny spots of red and green. The other blocks are in "Aunt Eliza's star design" (with a modified central square) of white, figured blacks, and grays. The triangles adjoining the central square and those outside the stars are dark gray, and the squares in the corners a lighter gray. The quilting, double parallel lines, is well done.[11]

A quilt believed to have a similar function is in the collection of the American Museum in Bath, England. Referred to as the Widow's Quilt, or Darts of Death, this quilt is made from pieced blocks of black darts alternating with plain white blocks, which are quilted in a lyre design. A black border surrounds the pieced design. The blocks are small, seven-and-a-half inches square, and the quilt is narrow, ninety-two by fifty-nine inches. There has been speculation that this denotes the solitary state of the sleeper, but the size could also indicate its use as a coffin cover. The quilt was found in New Jersey and dates from the mid-nineteenth centry.[12] This quilt, like many others of this type, is surrounded by a black border similar to the black-bordered handkerchiefs and stationary used by those in mourning.

Another type of mourning quilt is the Memory Quilt, made from the deceased's clothing. According to Carrie Hall, the pattern generally used was "Memory Wreath" and was "made of pieces of dresses worn by the dear departed, the name and date of death being embroidered in the white center square."[13] Memory quilts often contained religious or sentimental verses memorializing the deceased or comforting the living. Two examples of this type are the Susan Burr quilt and the Laura Mahan quilt.

The Burr quilt was made in 1844 in Mt. Holly, New Jersey, in memory of Susan N. Burr. The quilt incorporated pieces of Susan's clothing and was signed by her family and friends. The quilt is large, 94 by 96 1/2 inches, and is made in the Crossroads pattern. Twelve signatures are still visible, as is this inscription near the center of the quilt: "Think not though distant thou art/Thou cannot forgotten be/While memory lives within my heart/I will remember thee," and nearby: "To the memory of/Susan N. Burr/1844." The quilt descended in the family to the great-granddaughter of one of the signers, Anna Elton Rogers. The Rogers family were Quakers who settled in Burlington County, New Jersey, in the 1680s. While signature quilts in general were popular during the mid-nineteenth century, researcher Jessica Nicoll suggests that members of the Society of Friends found the idea of memory quilts particularly compelling.[14]

A second memory quilt, begun by Laura Mahan before her death in 1848, was finished by her stepmother, Sarah Mahan, in 1851. Quilt historian Ricky Clark tells the story of this quilt and the individuals involved in its history.[15] The quilt incorporates pieces from Laura's dresses, and the completed work commemorates Laura's life and death.

Forty-five of the blocks are inscribed by friends and family of the Mahans, primarily with biblical quotations and poems indicative of the sentimentalism of the day. The inscriptions also recognize the depth of Mrs. Mahan's loss; she was already a widow in 1843. Two blocks on the quilt record Sarah Mahan's departure from Oberlin, Ohio, a community which had been her base of support following her husband's death, to Belle Prairie, Minnesota, to teach in a mission school. The quilt was a testament to the love felt for Laura, just fourteen when she died. Additionally, it was a record of the community which had supported Sarah and her children and had been their home.

The practice of making a quilt from the clothing of the deceased was a fairly common practice. However, one unidentified widow, reversed this and made a quilt from her own mourning coat. The maker opened her black silk coat along the seams and made a mourning quilt to tell the story of her life with her husband. The central design is a coffin surrounding a vase with a drooping lily. Other design elements most likely illustrate aspects of the couple's life together, such as flags and a ship, while others symbolize their affection, paired hearts and spoons. The fabrics include pieces which may be from a wedding dress, and the maker embroidered a depiction of a man, perhaps to represent her husband. Fallen leaves and the lily symbolize death; the pansy, remembrance. Other embroidered motifs are not as easily understood, although the empty chair and pocket watch at the lower left appear to be additional symbols for an interrupted life. Writer Penny McMorris noted that the lines of embroidery, at time even and regular and at other times erratic, perhaps express the quiltmaker's changing moods.[16]

This unknown quiltmaker's manifestation of her grief over the loss of her husband is one of the most moving and eloquent of mourning statements. While one can only speculate as to their life together, we can surmise that the making of this spectacular object offered the maker solace and comfort in her grief and created a tangible memorial for her husband.

Quilts could and did have very practical purposes in association with the dead. A quilt might serve as temporary covering for the body, line the casket, or offer the only protection for the body in the cold ground. The latter practice was especially common during the Western migration in America in the mid- and late-nineteenth-century during which the mortality rate was high, and, on the treeless prairie, quilts often functioned as shroud and coffin combined.

Mrs. D. M. Burbank writes of much hardship and death on her journey west, to Utah:

> Then we went along the Platte River where we had cholora [sic]. Five died with it in our company. . . . My husband's wife Abby died with cholora and was buried without a coffin by the Platte River among the others. We had to go on in the morning and never saw their graves again. The night that Abby was buried the wolves were howling. It was awful to hear the dirt thrown on their bodies. A young lady and I were the only ones to wash and dress her with what we could find. Her underclothes and a nightgown. We sewed her up in a sheet and a quilt. That was all that could be done for her burial.[17]

Grace Snyder writes of the death of her first child:

> Bert made a coffin from a stout little ammunition box, and I told kind old Gramdma Houk where to look in my box cupboard for a lovely little featherstitched silk doll quilt that Aunt Ollie had given me years before. They wrapped the baby in the little quilt and laid her in the box. . . . Bert buried the tiny coffin in the yard at the foot of the little cottonwood tree. As soon as I was able, I went out and put a frame of narrow boards around the little grave.[18]

Sarah Leggett of Kountze, Texas pieced nine Lone Star quilts in black and white. She intended that each of her nine children be buried in his or her quilt. According to family tradition, "When a member of the family died, the kitchen door was removed (referred to as a 'cooling board'), placed on two chairs or sawhorses, and the body was placed on it and covered with the quilt while a pine coffin was constructed. When other family members died, they could be wrapped in the quilt—but it was to be buried with the son or daughter for whom it was made."[19] One quilt survives today because the son for whom it was made lived beyond the time of this burial tradition. The quilt remains in the family.

The "shroud quilt" or "coffin quilt" are the family names for a quilt made by Polly Taylor and Elizabeth Taylor Ruff which incorporates not only clothing of the deceased, but fabrics from shrouds and coffin linings. The quilt was made in Searcy County, Arkansas, about 1898, in memory of Polly's husband, Captain Benjamin Franklin Taylor. Taylor was ambushed and killed in the line of duty in Dover, Arkansas. The quilt incorporates names of other family members, some accompanied by birth and death dates. The center of the quilt forms a large square cut from remnants of the casket lining and edged with bits of lace from the same lining. "Pa's Shroud" is embroidered in the center. Remnants from Captain Taylor's burial clothing were also included in the quilt.

Referring to the quilt, Mrs. Opal Lee Taylor, a granddaughter of Mrs. Ruff, stated that "people in those days were sentimental about deaths and funerals. Caskets were made at home while the deceased was laid out on a cooling board and covered with a quilt, sheets were used in the summer. A silk handkerchief was placed over their face which was lifted for the last look." Mrs. Taylor remembers her father's statement upon the death of her younger brother, "Take the last look at your brother. The only time you will see him now is in heaven."[20]

Many of the quilts made to honor the dead were album quilts and signature quilts, both styles which were popular in the middle decades of the nineteenth century. In Baltimore, between 1846 and 1852 an exceptional and distinctive group of quilts emerged which have come to be known as Baltimore Album Quilts.[21] Within this tradition is a very fine quilt made by members of Eli Lilly's family at the time of his death in 1847.

Eli Lilly was born in Bristol, England in 1780, and immigrated

Figure 2. Detail of "Shroud Quilt" made by Polly Taylor and Elizabeth Taylor in memory of Benjamin Franklin Taylor, Searcy County, Arkansas, ca. 1898. 83 by 68 inches. Collection of Mrs. Opal Taylor.

to America with his parents in 1789. Lilly married three times, outliving each of his wives. He died December 3, 1847, in Baltimore. According to family tradition, at the time of his last illness his family gathered and made this quilt. It is signed by nine of Lilly's eleven children and their spouses, several friends, and by Lilly himself.

The quilt is beautifully appliqued with a variety of floral motifs, several of which are embellished with padding and embroidery. A swag border surrounds all four sides. Making the quilt provided a way for the family to gather, physically and symbolically, around Eli Lilly at his death. The quilt may have helped each member, including Lilly, prepare for his death.

Lilly signed the block with the lyre, an image often associated with death, but also a popular motif in the design vocabulary of seamstresses and other artists of the day. The quilt also provided a family record, commemorating the months the children and their spouses, many of whom had traveled long distances, spent together. The quilt has remained in the family, passed from daughter to daughter, to the present day. It continues to be a connection to that group of individuals who gathered around Eli Lilly in 1847.[22]

Several other album quilts of the period include a memorial to those departed, or a plea to those the maker left behind to "Remember Me." Some of the quilted memorials were similar to the painted and embroidered mourning pictures popular with young women at the beginning of the nineteenth century.

An album quilt from Rockland County, New York incorporates mourning symbols into one square. A male mourner, hat in hand, stands at a tombstone which is inscribed: "In memory/of/Edward H. Thompson/Died/June 3rd 1851 Aged 20 years/Blessed are they who die in the Lord." That block and several others are signed "John C. Gurnee" and on the back of the quilt is the inscription, "D. Thompson Gurnee". Approximately three dozen signatures, most of them North Rockland names, are penned on the quilt. Next to this block is a depiction of a building ringed by a cross, an anchor and hearts, symbols for faith, hope, and charity.[23]

Signature quilts sometimes included memorials along with other names and inscriptions. A quilt in the collection of the DAR Museum, made in Berks County, Pennsylvania, 1850–1851, contains a memorial inscription for a woman who died before the quilt's

Figure 3. Watercolor rendering of an Album Quilt, ca. 1850–60. All of the blocks carry a signature or initials with the exception of the central block which bears only "Mother" and "Remember Me." Index of American Design, National Gallery of Art, Washington, D.C.

completion, "Ellen B. Brimfield/Aged 77 years" and includes a verse from Longfellow's poem, *A Psalm of Life*: "Art is long and time is/ fleeting, And our hearts/tho stout and brave, still/like muffled drums are/beating funeral marches/to the Grave."[24] Signature quilts brought together people who were parted by death or distance. The quilts gave comfort and solace to their owners and helped to keep alive the memory of those departed.

The most famous of all quilts commemorating the dead is the Kentucky Graveyard Quilt made by Elizabeth Mitchell in 1839. Mr. and Mrs. Mitchell and their children moved from Pennsylvania, first to Ohio in 1831, then to Kentucky in 1834. While in Ohio, two of the Mitchells' sons died. After they moved, Mrs. Mitchell returned to Ohio to visit the boy's graves and experienced such grief that, upon returning home, she created her masterpiece. The quilt serves as a family record, a tangible memorial for her lost sons, and, hopefully, it helped her to cope with their deaths. Judging from its wear, it also served a practical function as a bedcover.

In the center of the quilt is the Mitchell family plot, with appliquéd coffins labeled with names of the deceased. Along the border of the quilt are additional coffins labeled with family names. Mrs. Mitchell planned to move these coffins into the plot, or cemetery, as her relatives died.[25]

Mrs. Mitchell's depiction of the family graveyard reflects this country's move away from the churchyard and public burial grounds of the eighteenth century to the formally planned, pastoral cemeteries of the nineteenth century. The earlier, disorganized lots gave way to enclosed burying grounds with an atmosphere of respose and protection from the harsh forces of the exterior world. Families also used metal railings to set apart their plots within public burying grounds.

Mrs. Mitchell's use of the burial ground as the the center of her quilt is both emotionally and visually compelling. She also uses the symbolism of flowers effectively. The rose or rosebud symbolizes death of the young and is a confession of love. In American art, a rose held downward or drooping from a broken stem meant an innocent life cut short. Roses, along with morning glories, were often included by painters and photographers in posthumous portraits of children. Mrs. Mitchell carefully embroidered roses trailing along the fence railings and entrance gate. Many of these blooms are drooping from their stems.[26]

Mrs. Mitchell expressed her grief through a very personal composition, although she incorporated accepted symbols for love and death. A number of twentieth-century quilters have taken objects from burials and imbued them with their own, personal, symbolism. Ribbons which adorn the floral sprays at funerals are collected, pressed, and used to create quilts which function as memorials and beautiful objects. The tradition has roots in both white and black communities, though the tradition may be more rural than urban.

Laura Lee, a black quilter in Chatham County, North Carolina, made a quilt from the funeral-flower ribbons of Judge Harry Horton. In discussing the quilt Mrs. Lee says, "He's dead, but I mean his wife saved the ribbons. She knew I made (quilts) and so she saved the ribbons. . . . And brought them. And I made that one and I remember what went into that one."[27] The ribbon quilt is composed of twenty squares with a pieced star at the center of each. While pink is the dominant color, yellow and red have been used to great effect in the pieced blocks. According to folklorist, Mary Anne McDonald, who has researched African-American quilts in Chatham County, Judge Horton was seen as a fair and reasonable man during the racial turbulence of the 1960s and was respected by the black community. For Mrs. Lee the quilt became a symbol of Judge and Mrs. Horton.[28]

Mrs. Lee also made a quilt from her son's funeral-flower ribbons. "She does not mention her feelings of grief at her son's death. . . yet . . . she frequently mentions the quilt she made from his funeral ribbons. This transformation from ribbons to quilt, from loss into useful object, enables Laura Lee to order her grieving within the framework of her life."[29]

Mrs. Bessie Alexander, a white quilter in Walker County, Alabama, made a quilt in 1972 from the funeral-flower ribbons of her mother-in-law. She was not aware of other quilts of this type, but said, "I just had so many ribbons, I wasn't sure what to do with them. A quilt was the only thing I could think of." In addition, she felt it was a "good way to keep something of sentimental value to you." Mrs. Alexander made one for herself and her husband, then two more, smaller ones, for each of her husband's sisters.[30]

Mrs. Alexander takes great pleasure in showing her quilt to others. It is a beautiful object, its lengths of richly-colored satin arranged unbroken by scissor-cut or elaborate pattern. Mrs. Alexander organized the colors symmetrically, beginning with deep lavender at the center of the quilt. The other colors—red, yellow, orange, and olive—fan out, in pairs, on either side of the first lavender ribbon.

The ribbon quilts have special meaning to the makers, commemorating a loved one and saving something associated with them. The ribbon quilts are related to other mourning quilts in memorializing the dead and in the comfort they provide the maker. The process of creating a whole from fragments is a healing activity and serves an important psychological function for those in mourning.

A contemporary quilter, Radka Donnell, discusses quilts she made commemorating the death of a young girl.

> I was commissioned to do two quilts using the clothes of a girl that had died. . . . It wasn't a mere question of [the mother] remembering her daughter. It was a question of putting her to rest. She needed some sort of ceremony that she could not find anywhere else and that the conventional funeral hadn't provided. . . . I was helping face the situation. And so I made the quilts and still had the feeling that the main thing had been her interaction with me and that the quilt was only a memorial to what happened between us."[31]

Another quiltmaker mentions the healing force of making a quilt. "The quilt was made just after my youngest brother was killed in a plane crash, a very sad event in my life, and this quilt [White Light] reflects my feelings. Also, making this quilt gave me much solace at the time."[32] Quilt artist Terrie Mangat created "E.B.'s New Pasture" after the death of her grandfather in 1982. The quilt incorporates loving memories of her grandfather, but also reflects conflict and resolution within the family and the love and deep bond between her son and grandfather. The quilt becomes both a memorial and a celebration.[33]

The AIDS epidemic and the scores of victims in its wake moved Cleve Jones of San Francisco to initiate a quilt project to illustrate the enormity of this epiemic. The NAMES Project Quilt, begun early in 1987, is an ongoing work which was first displayed in Washington, D.C., in October 1987, during the National March for Lesbian and

Figure 4. Some of the panels composing the NAMES Project Quilt on display in Birmingham, Alabama in 1989.

Gay Rights. The project involves stitching together cloth panels, measuring three by six feet, made by friends and families of AIDS victims.

The panels, made all over the country, memorialize those lost to the disease. Some of the memorials are stark statements, others are decorated with mementos from the lives of the deceased. When the quilt was first displayed it contained 1,920 panels. By early 1988, the quilt included 3,500 panels representing approximately thirteen per cent of the deaths from AIDS or Aids Related Complex.[34] The project has been an emotional one, but its healing forces are undeniable.

Mourning customs have become significantly less elaborate in the twentieth century. Mourning clothes were worn by women through World War I, but Geoffrey Gorer suggests that so many found themselves grieving the loss of loved ones during that time that the custom ceased to have much meaning.[35]

Romanticism of death and sentimental memorials to the deceased are no longer common or even considered appropriate. Mourners today are expected to accept their losses and go on with their lives as soon as possible. Viewed from the distance of the 1980s, we may consider nineteenth-century mourning customs and the objects associated with these customs, as overly sentimental, embarrassing, or bizarre. But, as one writer has noted, "mourning objects were external symbols of attachment and loss—and attachment continuing, in spite of loss."[36] Mourners in the twentieth century have, for the most part, abandoned visible adornments of mourning, but this does not mean our grief is any less powerful than in previous generations. The question is, did these visible expressions of mourning isolate the mourner and impede her integration back into the world around her, or did the separateness offer needed time for acceptance and accomodation to her loss?

It is possible that our century's de-emphasis on death makes the healing qualities associated with making a quilt in memory of a loved one even more important to those grieving. And, further, that mourning quilts, which have never been completely abandoned by quiltmakers, will become a more visible type made by today's quilters. The abilities that quilts have to bring people and memories together, to offer comfort to the makers, and to provide tangible memorials to the deceased are unmatched by any other medium.

A final example of the healing qualities of quilts are those made by quilters all over the country to memorialize the astronauts lost in the Challenger disaster. The explosion of the space shuttle Challenger on January 28, 1986, shocked and grieved people across the country. The tragedy propelled many quilters to come to terms with their grief through the creation of quilts. The efforts were spontaneous; none of the makers knew of others who, like them, needed an outlet for their sadness and loss.

Kathleen Francis, a quiltmaker in Wayne, Pennsylvania, states "When the Challenger exploded . . . more than the seven aboard were affected. . . . An entire nation grieved. In the grief I felt over the tragedy, an idea was born. To create a memorial for the seven and those they left behind. I knew from the very beginning that it had to be a positive statement. Since I am a quilter, it would, of course, be a quilt."[37] Ms. Francis and Linda L. Jesse created "They were Flying For Me—A Challenger Commemorative." © KWF1987 (based on a song by John Denver and used by permission).

The Francis/Jesse quilt is a variation of "Birds in the Air," adapted to include seven "birds" instead of five. Seven large stars are quilted across the quilt representing the seven astronauts, and smaller stars inside the larger stars represent the dependents they left behind. Fabric was chosen to best represent those aboard while other fabric and quilted designs symbolize spirit and light and the inspiration to keep reaching for our dreams. This quilt will hang in the Challenger Center in Washington, D.C., scheduled to open in 1992.

Ms. Francis discovered twelve other quilts made to commemorate the Challenger explosion. Several of the quilts employ the symbolism of birds in the air and stars and incorporate Christa McAuliffe's motto for the school children of America, "Reach for the Stars."[38]

California quiltmaker Linda Ballou made a quilt in subtle pastel shades, indicating a sunrise, with seven birds flying off in the distance. Ms. Ballou said, "This is not a hopeful quilt. It represents their spirits flying off never to be seen again. . . . I did not consciously think of that when I made it, it occurred to me after it was completed and I looked at it. . . . I have never made a quilt with such an emotional base to it."[39]

The Challenger disaster was a tremendous loss, one felt by the nation as a whole. When the nation loses a hero or suffers a grievous shock, there is often a need to express this sorrow in a tangible manner. According to Linda Ballou, "The loss (of a national hero) impacts your life so hard, you have to do something. I chose to make a quilt because that's the way I express my feelings best." These contemporary quiltmakers, many unconsciously, are continuing a tradition of accomodation to loss through the creation of quilted memorials.

Notes and References

1. Linda Grant DePauw and Conover Hunt, *Remember The Ladies: Women in America, 1750-1815* (New York: Viking, 1976), 43; Susan Burrows Swan, *Plain and Fancy: American Women and Their Needlework, 1750-1850* (New York: Holt, Rinehart and Winston, 1977), 181.
2. Sampler verses, tombstone epitaphs, musical lyrics, and literature provide excellent comparisons of the attitude change and resulting sentimentality in the early nineteenth century. For example, Rebecca Park's gravestone of the late eighteenth century reads in part, "Behold and see as you pass by/My fourteen children with me lie/Old or young

you soon must die/And turn to dust as well as I." DePauw and Hunt, *Remember the Ladies*, 38. Compare the above with "The Mother's Dream," published by Currier and Ives in the mid-nineteenth century with the verse: "The great Jehovah full of love;/An Angel bright did send,/And took my little harmless dove/To joys that never end."

3. DePauw and Hunt, *Remember the Ladies*, 40; Diana Williams Combs, "Commemoration in Mid-Nineteenth Century Georgia," *Georgia's Legacy: History Charted Through the Arts* (Athens: University of Georgia Press, 1985), 75–83.
4. "Editor's Table," *Godey's Lady's Book* 47 (July 1853): 84, quoted in Ricky Clark, "Fragile Families: Quilts as Kinship Bonds," *Quilt Digest* 5 (San Francisco: Quilt Digest Press, 1987), 19.
5. John Morley, *Death, Heaven and the Victorians* (London: Studio Vista Publications, 1971), 63.
6. Grace Snyder and Nellie Snyder Yost, *No Time on my Hands* (Caldwell, ID.: Caxton Printers, 1963), 316.
7. Lytton Strachey, *Queen Victoria* (New York: Harcourt, Brace, 1921), 402–3.
8. Ibid., 404.
9. Lou Taylor, *Mourning Dress: A Costume and Social History* (London: George Allen and Unwin, 1983), 122.
10. Taylor, *Mourning Dress*, 52–55. Taylor also states that among European artistocracy and the middle class, women's bed chambers were hung with yards of black cloth—floors, ceilings, walls, and furniture. The beds were draped with black hangings and sheets were stored and assembled when needed and loaned out to friends as necessary.
11. "Queries and Opinions," *The Magazine Antiques* 26, no. 1 (July 1934): 36.
12. Shiela Betterton, *Quilts and Coverlets from the American Museum in Britain* (London: Butler & Tanner, 1978), 38–39; Averil Colby, *Patchwork Quilts* (New York: Schribner's, 1965), 74.
13. Carrie Hall and Rose G. Kretsinger, *The Romance of the Patchwork Quilt in America* (Caldwell, ID.: Caxton Printers, 1935), 65, 77.
14. Jessica F. Nicoll, *Quilted for Friends: Delaware Valley Signature Quilts, 1840–1855* (Winterthur, DE: Henry Francis DuPont Winterthur Museum, 1986), 13.
15. Clark, "Fragile Families," 5–19.
16. Penny McMorris, *Crazy Quilts* (New York: E. P. Dutton, 1984), 86–87.
17. Mrs. D. M. Burbank, "Pioneer Journals," Special Collections no. Bt 8693: 53, University of Utah Library, information provided by Jeana Kimball of Salt Lake City.
18. Synder and Yost, 335; a similar story is recounted in Patricia Cooper

and Norma Bradley Buferd, *The Quilters: Women and Domestic Art* (Garden City, N.Y.: Anchor Press/Doubleday, 1978), 49.
19. Texas Heritage Quilt Society, *Texas Quilts, Texas Treasures* (Paducah, KY: American Quilter's Society, 1986), 36-37.
20. Mrs. Opal Lee Taylor, telephone interview by author, November, 1987.
21. Dena S. Katzenberg, *Baltimore Album Quilts* (Baltimore: Baltimore Museum of Art, 1982), 13-15.
22. Interview with Mrs. Louise Francke, June, 1987. The author is grateful to Mrs. Francke, Lilly's descendent and owner of the quilt, for the family history and personal research she so generously shared.
23. Mariruth Campbell, ed., *South of the Mountains* (New City, NY: Historical Society of Rockland County, 1976), cover and inside cover; Robert Bishop, *New Discoveries in American Quilts* (New York: E. P. Dutton, 1975), 82-3.
24. Gloria Seaman Allen, Curator, DAR Museum, Washington, D. C., interview with author, March 1987.
25. For further discussion and a photograph, see The Kentucky Quilt Project, *Kentucky Quilts, 1800-1900* (New York: Pantheon Books, 1982), 52-53.
26. Martha V. Pike and Janice Gray Armstrong, *A Time to Mourn: Expressions of Grief in Nineteenth Century America* (Stony Brook, N.Y.: The Museums At Stony Brook, 1981), 114-16; Combs, "Commemoration in Mid-Nineteenth Century Georgia," 79.
27. Mary Anne McDonald, "Symbols from Ribbons: Afro-American Funeral-Ribbon Quilts in Chatham County, North Carolina," in *Arts in Earnest: North Carolina Folklife*, eds. Daniel W. Patterson and Charles G. Zug, III (Durham: Duke University Press, 1989), 164-78.
28. Ibid, 164-65.
29. Ibid, 175-76.
30. Mrs. Bessie Alexander, interview with author, October 1987.
31. "Quilts in Women's Lives," a film by Pat Ferrero, quoted in Thomas L. Frye, ed., *American Quilts: A Handmade Legacy* (Oakland, CA.: Oakland Museum, 1981), 35.
32. Marilyn Davis, "The Contemporary American Quilter: A Portrait," in *Uncoverings 1981*, ed. Sally Garoutte (Mill Valley, CA: The American Quilt Study Group, 1982), 49-50.
33. Terrie Mangat, interview with author, October 1989.
34. Jeff Weinstein, "Names Carried into the Future: An AIDS Quilt Unfolds," *The Village Voice* (June 21, 1988): 19-23.
35. Geoffrey Gorer, *Death, Grief, and Mourning* (New York: Arno Press, 1977), xx-xxii, quoted in Patricia Campbell Warner, "Mourning and Memorial Jewelry of the Victorian Age," *Dress* 12 (1986): 60.

36. Warner, "Mourning and Memorial Jewelry," 59.
37. Kathleen Francis, "Challenge Quilts," *Quilting Today* 18 (Spring 1990).
38. Joseph J. Devanney, "The Legacy of the Challenger Quilts," *Quilt World* (December/January 1990): 56–7.
39. Linda Ballou, interview with author, January 1990.

SPECIAL PRESENTATION

A Tribute to Mariska Karasz (1898–1960)

Bets Ramsey

A new day for needlework artists dawned in the late 1940s when the Bertha Schaffer Gallery in New York chose to show the fabric collage and embroidery of Mariska Karasz. The exhibition signaled recognition of textile arts as being worthy of inclusion in the fine arts. But then, Mariska Karasz always was ahead of the times. To celebrate the pioneer efforts of this artist, her daughter, ceramist Solveig Cox, gave a special presentation about Karasz's life and works at the opening session of the 1989 American Quilt Study Group Seminar.

Mariska Karasz was born in Budapest, Hungary, in 1898, and came to America when she was sixteen years old. Almost immediately she began designing clothes and showing them at pleasant little openings in New York. Her work had the distinctive flair and detail of the truly creative designer.

Sometime later Mariska Karasz began doing needlework. She went to the abstract-expressionist painter, Hans Hoffman, and asked him how she could paint with a needle. "Just do it!" he said. From then on, the whole world was her source for design. She sent to France for every color of DMC thread. she looked for unusual fabric — muslin, linen, even woven horsehair and mesh potato bags — and every kind of thread, yarn, and string. Wherever she went she had an eye for unconventional materials to incorporate into her work.

Frequently she drew designs from the garden and landscape of her home in Brewster, New York, or from her travels to Mexico. She embroidered portraits of her daughters, Solveig and Rosamond, and stitched copies of their childhood drawings.

Bets Ramsey, Box 4146, Chattanooga, TN 37405.

As contemporary handcrafted furniture and accessories became fashionable, much of her work was designed for particular architectural spaces. These pieces took on a heavier, textural quality and larger proportions. One of her techniques was to couch down multiple strands of coarse threads with broad chain stitches. Indeed, the chain stitch in endless variation became her trademark.

Karasz exhibited her work in more than sixty shows. She was the author of *See and Sew, Design and Sew, Adventures in Stitches,* and a revised edition, *Adventures in Stitches and More Adventures—Fewer Stitches.* Her work is included in the collections of the Museum of Contemporary Crafts and the Cooper Hewitt Museum of the Smithsonian Institution, both in New York; the Cleveland Museum of Art; and many other institutions and private collections.

As guest needlework editor for *House Beautiful* in the 1950s, and with her work appearing in such magazines as *Woman's Day,* Karasz influenced hundreds of women by her innovative approach to needlework. At that time, fresh ideas in decorative arts were finally replacing attitudes held during the Colonial Revival period of the preceding decades. She was able to free embroiderers and others to experiment with their own modes instead of being slaves to the designs of "professionals." Such a simple plan as couching down randomly scattered threads and filling in the resulting shapes with stitches and embellishment offered an escape for novice fabric artists.

Mariska Karasz died in 1960, offering a legacy to many who are blessed by her adventurous spirit. A show of hands at the 1989 AQSG Seminar revealed dozens of lives influenced by the work of this remarkable woman.

Index

Album quilts, 146, 148
    sampler, 27, 31, **32**, 132. *See also* Baltimore album quilts; Friendship quilts; Signature quilts
Alexander, Bessie, 151–52
Alexander, Irene, 63
Anderson, Charlotte Warr, 118
Applique:
    by machine, 46–49, 50
    patterns, 34
        in album quilts, 34–35
Art deco style, 81, 82
Avery, Virginia, 108, 111, 112–13

Bailey, Elinor Peace, 114
Baker, Mrs. Daniel, 127
Ballets Russes, 83
Ballou, Linda, 155
Baltimore album quilts, 7–20, 31, 146
    books about, 14
    popularity, 9
    professional makers, 7, 9, 12, 13–14, 16, 17
    replicas, 17–18
    sales, 7–9, 15–16
    style, 8, 13, 16–17
Barbe, Amelia, 58–59
batting:
    cotton blanket, 132
    wool, 132, 135
Beard, Eleanor, 90
Benson, Bonnie, 105
Best, Frances, 55
Black, Narcissa, 49–50

Biedermier style, 93–94
Boag, Jane Patterson, 126
Boag, Marie, 129
Bodgett and Lerow (sewing machine company), 44
Bonesteel, Georgia, 105
Bordes, Marilyn, 9
Bottoms, Talula, 42
Boudoir:
    fashions, 84–89
    quilts, 89–92
    sets, 95
Boyce, Ann, 107
Boyer, Anna Margaret Strickrott, 131, 138
Bramble, Arthur Evans, 10, 11, 12, 20
Brimfield, Ellen B., 150
broderie perse, 31
Buffalo and Erie County Historical Society (BECHS), 123, 129, 133, 136
Burbank, Mrs. D. M., 145
Burr, Susan, 143–44
Burton-Dixie Co., 91–92
Butler, Gladys Boag, 126, 127–29

Cargo, Robert, 47
Carlin Comforts, 90
Challenger quilts, 154–55
Chamberlin, John, 8
Chamberlin, Rebecca, 8
Civil War, U. S., 28, 33
    use of sewing machine during, 39, 44–45

settlement of Nebraska after, 54, 57
Clark and Baker (sewing machine company), 44
Clark, Edward, 42-44
Clark, Ricky, 144
"Colonial-boudoir quilts," 83, 96
Colonial revival style, 82, 85, 90, 93-94, 96
Concord Fabrics, 102, 104, 106
Cottage industries, 89-91
Craft, Mathursa Jane, 47
Cult of Domesticity, 140
Cult of True Womanhood, 140

Deal, Susan, 118
DeWitt, Jeanne, 118-19
de Wolfe, Elsie, 86
Donnell, Radka, 152
Driscoll, Debbie, 107
Duff-Gordon, Lady ("Lucile"), 84
Dunton, Dr. William Rush, 14, 27, 142-43
 medical career, 13
 notebooks, 9-13, 21-23n
 Old Quilts, 7, 12, 13
 Quilt Dictionary, 12-13

Earley, Gayle, 118
Ehlers, Anna, 73, **73**
Ehlers, Lydia, 77
European styles, influence of, 81-85, 89, 92, 93-94
Evans (Ford), Mary
 birth date, 9, 12
 as professional quiltmaker, 7, 13, 14-15, 16
 signature, 19
 style attributed to, 11, 14, 16-17
 work attributed to, 7-9, 15-18
  applique blocks, 9-14, 21-23n
L'Exposition des Arts Decoratifs, 81

Fair, California State, 47
Fairfield/Concord Fashion Show, 104, 106-7, 109, 116-18
 guidelines, 114
 themes, 118
Fairfield Processing Corp., 102, 107, 115
Fashion shows, 102-4, 116-17
Feminist theory, 102-3, 105
Finley, Ruth E., 102-3, 105
Finley, Ruth E., 125, 126, 129
Flickinger, Julia Ann Cromer, 142-43
Foster, M. J., 47
Francis, Kathleen, 154-55
Franklin, Kate Mann, 94
Frasier, Belle, 61
Friendship quilts, 26, 27, 64, 65, 129. *See also* Album quilts; Signature quilts

Garments, contemporary quilted:
 Be a Sport, 118-19
 California Dreamin', 108
 Cruising the Planet, 108
 Crystal Transformation, 108
 Dance Electric, 108, 118
 Desert Moon Dream, 108
 Dreamin' Down Under, 108
 Extension, 108
 Fan-see This, 108
 Fantasia, 108
 Flyfishing Woman's Attire, 104
 God Save the Queen, 105
 Hot Ice, 108
 I Only Make Samplers, 105
 I Wanna Dance With Some Body, 108
 Jewel of India, 105
 Midnight Beauty, 105
 Midsummer Night's Dream, 107
 My Own Little Statement, 115
 Pavo Cristatus, 107

Remote Control I, 119
Silk Trade—Thank you, Marco Polo!, 118
Spatial Palatial Dancin'... The Black Hole Strut, 108
Super Star Fantasy, 108
Sweet Sixteen, 118
That Cotton Pickin' Garment, 105
There'll be a Hot Time in the Old Town Tonight, 108, 113, 116, 118
Things That Go Bump in the Night, 108, 118
Tropical Heat, 108
Vision Quest, 108
Wild Thing, 108, 118
Geise, Minnie, 63
Germany:
   fabric printed in, 130
   quilts made in, 58, 127, 131
Gleitman, George, 106
Goodenough, Florence I., 81, 95
Gorsuch, Elizabeth A., 9, 16
Grant, Helen, 95
Graves, Eliza Jane, 129, 138
Graves, Hannah, 132, 138
Great Depression, 59, 91-92
Griswold, Clarissa, 60
Grover and Baker (sewing machine company), 39, 40, 47

Haight, Sarah, 134
Hall, Carrie, 143
Hall, John W., 11, 23n
Hall, Lydia, 125, 133
Hanson, Lois, 66
Hearts and Hands (book), 14-15
Hervert, Jessie, 65
Hinrichs, Sophie, 60-61
Holstein, Jonathan, 46
Home Art Company, 29
Homestead Act, 54
Howe, Elias, 39

Hunt, Walter, 38
Huntington, Alceste, 41

Izolin down comforter, 92

Jahnke, Marie, 62
Jesse, Linda L., 154
Johnson, Abba Jane, 64-65

Katzenberg, Dena, 10, 12, 13-14
Keenan, Jean Wells, 118
Keller, Mary, 72, 75
Keller, Wes, 75
Kentucky Graveyard Quilt, 150-51
Kildare, Peg, 61, 65
Kirchmaier, Cora, 94
Kirchmaier, Hugo, 94
Kniffen, Fred B., 25, 26
Krevinghaus, Leola, **73**
Krevinghaus, Louise, 78
Krueger, Elma, 73, **73**

Labo, Eleanor, **73**
Labo, Margaret, **73**
LaCroix, Sophie T., 94
Ladies Aid Society, 69-79
LaFrenier, Dorothy, 72
LaFrenier, Lena, 72, 78
Lane, Carol Higley, 118
Lanigan, Sybil, 48
Lawrence, Mary Parks, 49
Lee, Laura, 151
Leggett, Sarah, 145
Lilly, Eli, family, 146-48
Lincoln (NE) Quilters Guild, 55
Lindhurst, Theresa, 73, 75

McCall Co., 92
McDonald, Mary Anne, 151
McGuire, Judith Brockenbrough, 44
MacKenzie, John P., 19
Mahan, Laura, 143
Mahan, Sarah, 144
"Male gaze," 105-6, 107, 108

Manakee, Mary E., 32
Mangat, Terrie, 152
Martin, Vickie, 105
Mason, Julia Smith, 123, 124-25, 129, 132-33
Masopust, Kim, 105, 107
Mathieson, Dick, 78
Mathieson, John, 76
Mathieson, Louise, 70, 72, **73**, 76, 77
Maxwell, Ellen, 59
Memory quilts, 143-44, **147**
Meyer, Lillian, 72, **73**
Miller, Priscilla, 106, 117
Mitchell, Elizabeth, 150
Models, fashion, 107-8, 110, 114, 116-17
Morelock, Jane Richey, 48
Mountain Mist batting wrappers, 69
Mourning:
  customs, 140-42
  pictures, 139
  quilts, 142-43, **149**
Mulvey, Laura, 105-6

NAMES Project Quilt, 152-53, **153**
Newkirk, Mary Catherine Ray, 65
Norris, Julia Pickett, 125, 130, 132, 133, 138
Norris, Fred, 125, 133, 138

Orlofsky, Patsy and Myron, 9
Orr, Ann, 94

Palmer Brothers Co., 91
Palmer, Louise, **73**
Palmer, Nettie, **73**
Partridge, Elizabeth, 129
Patchwork, modified, 92-93
Peck, Jessie Farrall, 125, 134
Peters, Edna, **73**
Pickell, Sylvia, 18
Pickett, Elizabeth Havens, 124, 138
Pickett, Eliza Jane Graves, 132, 138
Pickett, Martha Jane Armstrong, 129, 138
Poiret, Paul, 84
Pool, Mary J., 15
Pool, Sarah, 15
Powers, Harriet, 49
Practical Patchwork Co., 95
Prange, Helena Hinrichs, 60-61
Prentice, Hepzibah, 135

Quilt-as-you-go, 46-47
Quilt:
  collections, 123, 125
  Expo Europa, 104, 106, 117
  kits, 76, 95
  patterns, sources for, 75
  prices, 90, 91-92
  Projects, 27, 34, 35
    Nebraska, 55
    procedure, 55-56
  revival, 103, 104
Quilting:
  bees, 71, 106
  by church groups, 66, 69-79, 133
  for hire, 74
  machine, 46-47, 48, 49
Quiltmakers:
  children as, 61
  Nebraska
    ages of, 62-63
    ethnic origins, 57
    fabric sources, 64
    occupations, 56-57
    pattern sources, 64
    productivity, 63
    religious affiliations, 57-58
  professional, 7, 9, 12, 13-14, 16, 17
Quiltmaking:
  motivations for, 58-60, 71, 139, 152, 155
Quilts:
  as artifacts, 26, 67
  appliqued, 123
  as occupational therapy, 13

Index

date-inscribed, 27
embroidered, 123, 151
fabrics in:
    rayon, 82, 92
    silk, 82, 89, 90, 92
from clothing of deceased, 144
from funeral ribbons, 151–52
for marriage, 131
outline-embroidered, 28
Quaker (Society of Friends), 144
sales of, 7–9, 15–16
slave-made, 48
used in burial, 145–46
whole-cloth, 123, 134–35
Quilts or quilt patterns, named:
  Basket, 58
    Cherry, 49
    French, 94–95
  Birds in the Air, 154–55
  Blind Man's Fancy, 127
  Caesar's Crown, 127
  Cactus Rose border, 135
  Castile quilt, 125, 134
  Charter Oak, 134
  Chimney Sweep, 129, **130**
  Chinese Coin, 132
  City Springs block, 10–11, 12–13, 10
  Cockscomb and Currant, 48–49
  Colonial Girl, 72
  Crazy quilt, 59, 60, 65, 127
  Crossroads, 143
  Darts of Death, 143
  Delectable Mountains, 135, **136**
  Double Wedding Ring, 64, 75
  Dresden Plate, 64
  Eagle, 47
  Feathered Star, 47
  Fleur-de-lis, 34
  Flying Geese sashing, 127
  Four patch, 61, 132
  Friendship, 64
  Grade Crossing, 133
  Grandmother's Flower Garden, 64
  Hovering Hawks, 133
  Irish Chain:
    Double, 129
    Single, 75
  Jacob's Ladder, 133
    Double, 129
  Lincoln quilt, 129
  Log Cabin, 50, 64
    Barnraising, 64
  Lone Star, 75, 145
    Gone Crazy, 129
  Shroud quilt, 146, **147**
  Silhouette Wreath, 18
  Star of Bethlehme, 126
  Sunbonnet Sue, 64
  Sunburst, 129
  They Were Flying For Me, 154–55
  Trip Around the World, 59
  Tulip, 48
  Tumbling Blocks, 127
  Variable Star, 132
  Wagon Tracks, 133
  Whig Rose, 35
  Widow's quilt, 143
  Wine Glass, 132
  Memory Wreath, 143
  Mexican Rose, 34
  Midnight Star, 143
  Nine patch, 64
  Oak Leaf and Reel, 34, 134
  Overall Boys, 64
  Pan-American Penny Blocks, 127, **128**
  Pineapple, 50, **50**, 135
  Pine Tree, 47
  Princess Feather, 35, 48
  Railroad Crossing, 133
  Red Woven Basket of Flowers, 18
  Rob Peter to Pay Paul:
    Complex Version, 130, **131**
    Hearts Version, 124
    Hexagon Version, 129
  Ruched Rose Lyre, 18

Rabe, Clara, 72, 73, **73**, 77–78
Rabe, Emma, 75
Rabe, Otto, 75
Rainbow Quilt Company, 29
Reinstein collection, 123, 125–27, 129, 134, 135
Reinstein, Anna, 126, 127
Reinstein, Victor, 125–26, 127
Reinstein, Julia Anna, 126, 133
Reinstein, Julia Boyer:
    awards, 135
    as collector, 123, 126–27, 129, 134, **136**
    education, 125, 126
    family, 124, 125
    as historian, 123
    as lecturer, 126, 130
    marriage, 125
    as preservationist, 123, 124, 135–36
    as quiltmaker, 133
Rogers, Anna Elton, 144
Ruff, Elizabeth Taylor, 146

Schockey, Gertrude, 92
Schule, Mrs., 127
Schum, Rev. Alfred, 70, 72
Schum, Irma, 70–72
Scudder, Gertrude, 59
Sewing machine:
    ability to use, 40
    cost, 41, 43
    invention, 38–39
    learning to use, 42, 45, 46
    manufacturers, 44
    marketing of, 39–44, **41**
    use of, by quiltmakers, 38, 44, 46–51
Sewing Machine Combination, 39
Shaffer, Mrs. M. E., 47
Signature quilts, 26, 65, 129, 143, 146–150. *See also* Friendship quilts; Album quilts.
    as artifacts. 25, 35
    books about, 27–28

definition, 27
distribution of, 30–33
earliest dates, 28
incidence of, **29**
popularity, 27–28
as records, 26
revival, 28
Singer, I. M., and Co., 39, 40, 42–44, 47
Singer, Isaac Merritt, 38, 39
Slaughter, Amanda, 43
Sliver, Elizabeth, 18, 19
Smith, Agnes Pickett, 124, 132, 138
Snyder, Grace, 141, 145
Stapley, Mr., 127
Sterbak, Jana, 119
Strickrott, Anna Marie Strauss, 130, 138
Strickrott, John Christopher, 130
Symbolism:
    on grave markers, 140
    in mourning quilts, 144, 148, 150–51
    in needlework, 139

Taylor, Opal Lee, 146
Taylor, Polly, 146
Thomsen, Kathryn, 66
Triplette, Ardyth, 62
Twining, Mary Arnold, 123–24

Updegraf, Mary, 7–8, 16, 19

Van Derhagen, Mrs., 135
Victoria, Queen of England, 141–42
Victorian styles, 82, 85, 89, 96

Waldron, Jane D., 125, 134
Walker, Leroy, 57
Webster, Marie, 94–95
Weidlich, Lorre Marie, 103
Weisenthal, Charles, 38
Weitz, Maria, 127
Welty, Elizabeth, 41

Wheeler and Wilson (sewing machine company), 39, 42, 44
Wicker, Maria, 42
Wilder, Donna, 118
Wilkins, Achsah Goodwin, 14
Wilkinson, Ona, 90
Willcox and Gibbs (sewing machine company), 44
Witte, Ida, 72, **73**, 78
Witte, Minnie, 73, **73**, 74
Witte, Paul, 74
Witte, Sarah, 72, 73, 76
Women:
   body image, 110-11, 114-15
   diaries, 44
   magazines, 40-41, 46, 48, 81, 84-96
   roles, 103, 105-6, 108, 111-13, 140
World War II, 76
Worth of Paris, 45

Young, Genevieve, 59

The American Quilt Study Group is a nonprofit organization devoted to uncovering and disseminating the history of quiltmaking as a significant part of American art and culture. AQSG encourages and supports research on quilts, quiltmaking, quiltmakers, and the textiles and materials of quilts. Membership and participation are open to all interested persons. For further information, contact the American Quilt Study Group, 660 Mission Street, Suite 400, San Francisco, CA 94105.